The Arrival of the Promise Land

The Arrival of the Promise Land

Bringing "YOU" to a Place Where Serenity, Prosperity and Magic Reign Supreme.

Katherine Irvin

katherinerhp@gmail.com
kat13616@yahoo.com
Website: www.kmrieds.com

Copyright © 2014 by Katherine Irvin.

ISBN: Softcover   978-1-4990-3648-0
          eBook   978-1-4990-3647-3

All rights reserved. No part of this book may be reproduced or transmitted in any form or by any means, electronic or mechanical, including photocopying, recording, or by any information storage and retrieval system, without permission in writing from the copyright owner.

Any people depicted in stock imagery provided by Getty Images are models, and such images are being used for illustrative purposes only.
Certain stock imagery © Getty Images.

Print information available on the last page.

Rev. date: 08/02/2019

To order additional copies of this book, contact:
Xlibris
1-888-795-4274
www.Xlibris.com
Orders@Xlibris.com
635536

Table of Contents

Dedication vii
The Author Autobiography ix
Introduction xv
Film Synopsis 1
Problem Statement #1 30
Let's Analyze Occurrences That's Out of this World 35
The Introduction: Historical Origin and Way of life of Humanity 38
Historical Identity and Way of life of the Indigenous Negro American Population 40
Christopher Columbus and the UFO 47
Why was the Constitution, Congress and the Declaration formed? 53
The Atlantic Slave Trade Story is the Biggest American Lie Ever Written in Human History! 57
10 Million Africans Stolen from Africa is Impossible! 65
The Current Grievance Statement & Solution Proposal- To the Governor of the Federal Reserve Systems 67
New Alternative Reparation Solution Plans,
for African American BILL ACT 75
Indigenous Negro Constitutional Law Decree 85
An Introduction to the Promise Land Company Public Social Services 97
The Company! The Promise Land Community Initiatives! 99
Katherine's Syfy Film Trilogy Bonus! 129
UFO/Alien Encounters 135
Conclusion 145

The Arrival of the Promise Land

This book is dedicated to anyone who wishes to live in a Real Magical "Promise Land" Community.

But first... On this Day of 6/16/2019; Time 6:16 Am

We the People ask our Soul Creators to bring the Arrival of the Promise Land to America. We the People" Are tired, we feel unhinged about living in an overruled dysfunctional governmental society. We fear for the future of our loved ones.

Our greatest idea and visions have always been less forthcoming due to various corrupt policy Laws that are woven within the fabric of our society. And, have made life as a virtual living Hell for 99% of Americans.

Much respect and acknowledgment to the <u>Ones that Brought us Down Here</u>. Our Intentions are Greatly Positive, and we Grateful for the Everlasting Power Given to us so that we may Create the "Promise Land" as a Reality for ALL.

My Warmest Gratitude,

"Katherine Irvin"

The Author Autobiography

Ms. Katherine Irvin, Mother of four Beautiful Children. She was born in Harvey IL, on April 10, 1968. Together with her Mother and Father and 3 siblings, they grew up in Grand Rapids Michigan. Her Father served in the Military around 1945 and then later worked in Steel Mill Factories. He did not believe in Religion, God, Church or Jesus and couldn't stand Black people who were considered as "Coons"

Mother was young who lived a hard life through years of Severe Child Abuse and Neglect by her own mother (Katherine's grandmother) as they lived through Poverty, Racism and Government Corruption. [Katherine learned of this at age 18] Katherine's mother is a Wonderful and Beautiful homemaker. She was more into the belief of Metaphysics, Spirituality, and Karma. This allowed young Katherine and her 3 siblings to grow up with an open conscious mind. She had a fun exciting childhood rather Magical she might say. Her Parents celebrated every Holiday, birthdays and would often take the whole family on camping fishing trips, Drive-In Theaters, and Carnivals. Mother would play all sort of Board games or take trips to the Museums or various events.

Things turned for the worst when Katherine turned 18 years old. From the divorce of her parents forced them to move to Phoenix Arizona. Katherine stayed in AZ for 13 years and had two small children of her own. She was living in poverty and faced homelessness. She decides to move with her children to Los Angeles California in search of a better life. Only too ended up in a 20-year struggle of Homelessness, Poverty, Racism and government corruption.

Despite the of the Struggle, Katherine has over 30 years of extensive research and Knowledge of her Ancient Culture as well as African and European History. Her major is Urban Planning & Economic Development. Her goal is to one day own her own Home with lots of Land to build a large food garden and animal sanctuary in a prosperous safe community of her own creative development.

Since her earliest childhood, Katherine has always envisioned herself creating Communities of Great Beauty, Safety, Prosperity, Enlightenment and Magic.

Strangely enough, she somehow knew at the early age of 5-years old. That there was something seriously wrong with the Planet. She knew that certain people were suffering more than others even though she hasn't heard of it. She also knew there was something extremely Powerful that was guiding her throughout her life. Even though no one else informed her of this. Yet somehow, she knew was being guided by "Knowingness". And through this knowledge, she knew she had to pray or Summons or call upon to a Higher Soul Source" as she would call it. She has prayed for the ability to see things most people can't see. And to be fully <u>Aware of things</u> that most people are NOT aware of but <u>should be aware of</u>.

From the age of five through twelve years old she has prayed for the knowledge to transform the worst impoverished Inner-city areas throughout America into communities most people would call the "Promise Land" Communities neighborhoods so incredibly made that it's "Worth Fighting For" a place where all people can "Truly" live a Beautiful Free and Advanced Prosperous Life" Throughout her adulthood she often thinks that some of her ideas and knowledge to change the world was contributed to "Otherworldly" Encounters. That she remembers happening throughout her life. This knowledge has grown and developed into a vision of the Greatest Urban Community and Economic Development Plan this world has ever seen!

Unfortunately, Katherine would be her own first client, since the age of 19, she was forced to deal with homelessness and government corruption such as; the relentless Police Brutality and Stalking going on with Black males. Katherine fears for the safety of her children particularly her 17-year-old son who suffers from Autism. (Autism caused by the U.S. Government HHS Mandatory Vaccination Shots). Katherine and her children have suffered for over 20- years under homelessness due to the high cost of living, low paying Job wages and lack of permanent housing or homeownership programs. She's been living in and out of various Homeless and Transitional housing Shelters in some of the worst government facilities in Arizona and California State.

For many years she's searched for suitable business opportunities to start a business or to buy a home. She has applied at every Government Social Service Programs known to man. And, none have offered any real effective solutions. She doesn't just speak for herself; she speaks for millions of people across America who are suffering from Nationwide Racism and Government Corruption.

Katherine has years of extensive research and Knowledge of her Ancient Culture. According to Katherine's Great, Great Grandparents none of these criminal law policies that were all dealing with today ever existed prior to 1619-1790. More importantly, Katherine and Millions of other people of ALL Races are starting to realize a shocking revelation, an absolute Crime Kicker of unimaginable apportions! A small Portion of her shocking discovery is the fact that the United States Government, Congress, have always been fully aware that millions of Black People like Katherine are in fact <u>Indigenous to America</u>!!

Throughout her adult life has made her realize that most things our society has taught us to believe have all been one Big Gigantic LIE. Katherine has noticed the People" are starting to realize a long history of Law policies. That is implement turned out to be extremely fraudulent and deadly. Not just for Black Indigenous Americans but for all American people. She begins to realize that 90% of all Black people living in America, (Great, Great Parents) were not kidnapped from Africa at all. But had thriving "Advanced Civilizations" throughout America, Mexico, Haiti, Cuba, Porta Rica, to South America that predates while over 40,000 to 3 Million years ago!

Realizing that most of the heartache, misery, stress and mental anguish stemming from poverty could've all have been prevented. Any person who is Indigenous in their Country should never be put in a situation where they are forced to being ruled over by a foreign government entity. Katherine has come to realize that No one should be forced to pay thousands if not millions of dollars for their own "Inherited" land and home! And as a result, of these unwarranted policy laws is the #1 cause of Poverty, Homelessness, Crimes, and Severe Mental Stress in America. These unwarranted government Law Polices have virtually cripple every single Black Indigenous family in America. Making our way of life the most Dangerous and Dysfunctional living environment in the world.

Throughout Katherine's overwhelming adversity she has gained tremendous knowledge to solve the most important problems that exist today. And has put together her World Changing Idea into (1) Indigenous Negro American Law Decree and (3) different Business Project Plans. Together they are designed to eliminating the biggest problems that exist today while providing the greatest solution to transform impoverished Urban Neighborhoods. Communities of Beauty, Prosperity, Safety, Enlightenment, and Sustainability.

Since 2007 She has founded two companies called "The Robin Hood Project Inc and Katherine's Magical Kingdom LLC. Both Company names have been changed to; <u>S.S.H.E.A- Successful Service Housing & Educational Arena's Inc</u>. and <u>K.M.R.C.E.D. -Katherine's Magical Revitalization Community & Economic Development Inc</u>. Both Companies are designed to create **Promise Land Style** Communities. Throughout America's Urban Inner core and certain Rural areas where the poverty level is at 99%. Her planned development was designed and written for the People" who work to do "Good" in this World, Business Investors, Film Directors, Agents, Producers, and the United States Senate, Legislation, Congress Assembled and the President of the United States.

Since 2008 Katherine has Presented her Companies Life Changing "Business Plans" to former *President William Jefferson Clinton) *California Senator Diane Feinstein through April 2007-2018) *Congresswoman Maxine Waters 2010) President Barack Obama in 2009 – 2013) *California Governor Jerry Brown 2009 -2017) *Local Congressmen Paul Cook 2016) *Local Legislation Assembly 2017) *The Governors of the Federal Reserve System September 2018-2019) U.S. Department of Community Housing and Economic development January 2019) Philanthropist Evenly Rothchild's) March 2019- Small Business Administration.

All government officials have notified Katherine, through letters of acknowledge and local business meetings. And all have rejected her idea suggesting that she apply for Government Grants and Banking Loans.

Katherine informed them all that it would be virtually impossible given the circumstances, in which their U.S. Policy Law is written and carried out. Like so; "In order to be granted any Government Grant, Banking Business loan or to receive funding from any Small Business Administration. These following credentials must be present during any Loan Application process.

- ✓ Half of the funds that are being requested must be in your Bank Account.
- ✓ Certain valuable Collateral must be added.
- ✓ The Business itself must be successfully operating 2- years prior.
- ✓ An Annual Tax fee of $873.00 dollars is required to own a Corporation.
- ✓ Must have a perfect credit score of 720-800
- ✓ Four References from successful Business Partnerships.

Katherine has informed them that their business loan policy requirements would be nearly impossible for an average impoverished person to achieve in starting a business. This is partly the reason why <u>Only 3.8%</u> of the so-called African Americans are business owners.

No government official has given any response back to Katherine's return explanation and request. Despite the non-compliance, bias complacency of the United States government officials there is still some hope.

All is NOT Lost...

Katherine may have found another way to obtain financial Support in the Marketing, Sale, and Promotion of her amazing One-of-A-Kind Community and Economic Development Plan. This Plan is TREMENDOUS. Part of her community development service is to create a major motion picture film so amazing it could change the world!

Based on this book could create a Spectacular Featured Film that is also made for the Most Exciting and Intriguing TV Trilogy Series!! At the beginning of this Book will show the unique Featured Film Synopsis and Treatment! It's to give the American Audience members a Fantasy Thrill/ Adventure, from a Realistic Urban Inner-city point of view. Indeed, to show America the full spectrum of our Promise Land Communities will ultimately become a reality for all humanity.

Introduction

Great News Everyone! The Creator of the Promise Land is Finally Here!

A fully complete Promise Land Community is similar in nature to a Highly Advanced Garden of Eden > meets< Theme Park Heaven! With of course the exception that it's more appropriate to be fully clothed in the "Garden of Eden". You can also eat whatever fruit you like without having to go to hell or be condemned for it. And we do not have any talking snakes in the garden, nor do we have any kind of religions, cults, guns, kidnapping, prisons, murders, rapist, pedophiles, crime, theft, government corruption nor tyranny. Nonsense like that could Never exist in our Promise Land Communities. We plan on building the most amazing Promise Land Style Communities Nearby Urban areas where the poverty level is at 99%.

> Our Mission is to create a Better American Country that
> Caters to the Most Important Needs of the People.

Our Extraordinary Business Services Represents or Resembles the Following;

- ❖ Heaven on Earth
- ❖ The Promise Land
- ❖ Innovative Reparation Initiatives.
- ❖ The Arrival of the Promise Land Company Services.
- ❖ Combing Amazing Theme Parks & Community Housing Together.

Why, "The Arrival of the Promise Land"?

Because criminal decisions that were made in the past continue to cause the lives of Millions in our present. From the perspective of an Indigenous Negro Point of view; Our Country was illegally taken over by Foreign" Groups. These "Foreign" groups represent the United State Federal Government Business Corporation. No Government is supposed to dictate how a community should live out the rest of its life. Especially if that Dictatorship" is "Foreign" and altogether different reasoning of Cultural perspective and Reality.

The United States Government is the only government that outlawed itself by being completely void of all *Logical Reasoning, *Common Sense and *Authoritative Inheritance. It's the three most important element that any government body must have when governing over its Indigenous country. And because of this void has ultimately caused the worst 200 to 400-year Take-Over" in Human History. Millions of Indigenous Negro Americans and the African Americans are the present Victims and the rightful Heirs of their potential Land, Home, and Businesses. [Certain White people are also Victims of Slavery as well] Explained in my Book "The Arrival to the Promise Land"

We are currently living in a Hellish existence due to the near annihilation of our Great, Great Indigenous Grand Parents. They Did NOT sign any agreement for their Country to be taken over by anyone other than themselves!!! We are their Descendants; we are here to establish Prosperous, Safe and Sustainable Communities. That would've been implemented Centuries ago if it were not for the Foreign take-over that began in our Lands in 1619 and Increased in size in 1945 -2019

In a nutshell, we are in the business of...

"Combining Amazing Theme Parks & Community Housing Together!

Our goal is to Bring Great People together, in Fantastical Places" Wonderful places where People can now choose their favorite Neighborhood Theme Park to visit. Amazing Communities where you can also fix your own Law Policy. Policies that are right for You, and your family's personal needs and situation. Urban Communities with unlimited Enrichment opportunities for the "Wellbeing, Happiness, Safety and Sustainability for generations to come. Based on the Company's Constitutional Indigenous Negro Law Decree!

This book speaks to those who can see that a Much Better Life Approaches!

It gives the reader Important information that is Straight forward "Raw" and Knowledgeable about Who, How, Where or When the Promise Land will be developed in a Neighborhood near You! But importantly enough, in order to create or live in the Promise Land, one must know its own history. In order to "Truly" move forward in life. You must know where you came from in life. We all must get educated no matter what race or nationality we are. We must learn and Know our INDIGENOUS Identity First! This would eliminate a lot of the confusion on who has the Original Authoritative Right to Govern over its own Country.

We outline Accurate Historical Identity Information [for research and educational purposes only] that also comes with our Company's Rule of Law Policy called "The Promise Land, Indigenous Negro Constitutional Law Decree" A comprehensive plan to develop Promise Land Style Communities throughout America. We also outline the current Problem Statement that we are all dealing with today. While providing the Greatest Solution to that problem.

The Film Treatment of the book is for the best interest of the Director, Producers and Agent/Manager. At the end of this Book, is an additional Film Treatment entitled "Katherine's Sci-fi Series Bonus!" Also, for the Public interest in the Paranormal. I added various UFO and Alien Stories, pick out which one of the Alien Encounters You Think Really Happened?

So, without further ado, I Present the Film Synopsis and the Film Treatment.

Film Synopsis

"The Arrival of the Promise Land"

This Dramatic, Sci-fi Fantasy film has an awe-inspiring "Twist."

Logline

America hangs in the balance between Truth and Tyranny. Only the help of "Other Worldly Forces" can bring the Promise Land to America'

<u>**Characters**</u> First 5 Scenes of the Film.

LAMAR, male (College Student age 25) lives in the worst crime infested inner-city of Los Angeles, CA. He finds out that it's not just gang members that are committing murders, but a far more sinister act is afoot — running from gang violence. He finds himself in another Dimension of the "Promise Land."

JOSH, White male (High schooler, age 17 Skateboarder) Blond or Brown hair, blue eyes. Josh is a good-hearted person. He was brutally beaten by Police, sending him to the hospital. Courts later sentence Teen to a

Juvenile detention center. But fate would bring him into another Dimension of the "Promise Land."

KEITH, (Sells Marijuana age 30) Ex-Gang member who looks for a fast buck to pay the bills. He and his friends find themselves in a sinister government plot sending them to prison. Keith meets two "Galactic Beings" disguised as prison inmates, that leads him and others into the "Promise Land."

VICTORIA, (Job Seeker age 33, living in Los Angeles California) a Mother of two children of an abusive relationship with the baby's father. She is gripped by poverty, homelessness and government corruption. Unaware that she's about to be guided into the "Promise Land."

MALTA, NAGUS and KAH, three Beautiful Galactic Giant Women, they stand over 16ft, from the HIGH COUNCIL OF SEVEN. These women are from a Planet near Sirius C. They know the time is near for their Bloodline Relatives to receive their full Power and Conscious. They know that a greater Galactic Evil is nearby.

ACT 1

The Arrival of the Promise Land focuses on the American struggle of four individuals from different backgrounds and situations. They must overcome devastating adversities dealing with poverty, gang violence, homelessness, Police Brutality, and Government Deceit and Corruption. The dire living conditions in their neighborhood are screaming for a solution! One woman named Victoria unknowingly holds the key within her DNA, that could unleash everlasting Power, Magic, Transformation and High Consciousness to all Inner-city areas. But only through the help of her of long- lost Galactic Family-Malta, Nagus and Kah. They must find Victoria before the EVIL forces of TAK-CONIANS known as the TAK-CONS find her.

The people and Earth itself are illegally cut off, cloaked and hidden away from the rest of the galaxy. The People's link to their Galactic higher Selves is in their Chakras. But their Chakras has been tampered with by evil galactic forces of the "Tak-conians and their connections with the U.S. Department of HHS, CDC, Food and Drugs administration. The Tak-cons have illegally appointed themselves as the "Gate Keepers" their Allies are the Governments of Earth. They have been holding the People Hostage and using them like Cattle, a food source, feeding on their soul energy. They cannot survive without creating misery, devastating bloodshed, oppression, and tyranny.

ACT 2

For eons, the High Galactic Council of Seven has been in search of their descendants throughout the Galaxies. They have no idea that their long-lost relatives are on Earth. Until the galactic women Malta, Nagus, and Kah uncover a deep dark secret so treasonous it would change the Universe forever!

Three galactic women have secretly uncovered this most treasonous crime ever recorded. But they must keep the secret hidden until they can convince their people and the High Galactic Council to release the people of earth from their bondage and oppression. The evil Tak-cons heard about their untimely discovery and they will stop at nothing to keep their secret hidden. The galactic chase is on and the battle begins between the Tak-conians and Council of Seven's army.

The Galactic battle is then suddenly unleashed on earth bursting through the clouds and onto the unsuspecting people. sending the CDC government to unleash a deadly virus into the atmosphere to stop the Galactic Council of seven of giving Victoria and the people the greatest power on earth.

ACT 3

The entire Country is being exposed by a deadly virus from the CDC. During the battle between Earth and Sky Malta, Nagus, and Kah finally find their descendant and desperately attempt to befriend Victoria to gain her trust. Once Victoria begins to understand what's happening, she then accepts the power. But Victoria is infected by the Plague and has no strength. Later she is suddenly rejuvenated by the Powers are given to her from the Galactic Council. She decides to go back in time to save the people that lost their lives and succumbed to poverty. She goes 10 years back leading the suffering people into the Promise Land.

She then thinks of the ATLANTIC SLAVE TRADE. And, goes back 400 years unleashing the Promise Land throughout America. And, finds out that most enslaved people can't even conceive of breaking free to enter the Promise Land. Therefore, it doesn't exist for those who can't conceive of it.

Victoria fast forwards herself back to 2020 And is met up with Lamar, Josh, and Keith together, they work as Community Leaders, Mentors, Teachers, Safety Leaders, and Guardians, etc., to open the minds of those who are mentally trapped.

The streets of the worst inner cities suddenly open an invisible doorway to another dimension. Eye-opening for the people who are suffering from severe poverty, oppression, government injustices. Ultimately changing people from being weak with low self-esteem and fearful. Into a people of tremendous Strength, Confidence and Magic Powerful Abilities. Thousands of people Chakra system has an interactive link into the higher dimensions of the Promise Land. It is still evil on earth but, this time, Good and Evil are on an even playing field. Earth is now a world of Superheroes and Villains alike.

THE END

I hope you enjoyed the Synopsis.
The Film Treatment is Next.

THE ARRIVAL OF THE PROMISE LAND
A TREATMENT FOR A FEATURE FILM SCREENPLAY

Featured Film Treatment
WRITTEN BY
KATHERINE IRVIN

[ACTION]

[Black Screen. Words Appear]
"What is the use of a God who only Dwells in Heaven?"

EXT. The year is 2020. Los Angeles Ghetto Neighborhood. Night.

[BLACK SCREEN]
The sound of heavy frantic breathing, sounds of running, scurrying on concrete pavement, running person tripping over what sounds like a garbage can, papers are raffling, dogs barking.

LAMAR

Example Photo

Black male, sweaty, good looking, wearing College style clothing with a backpack over his shoulders. He is frantically running, struggling to stay on his feet, he accidentally drops his books and papers leaving it in the wind and on the sidewalk of a crime infested neighborhood of Los Angeles. Running for his life from unknown gang violence.

[4 BLACK MALES GANG MEMBERS ages range from 17 to 23] Two of the Gang men are running close behind Lamar down the neighborhood sidewalk. One of the gang men stops takes aim and fires a shot. Hitting Lamar in the Arm, Lamar yells out in pain

grabbing his arm while rushing around the corner of an abandon Liquor store building. Lamar is out of breath leans up against the corner street light pole to catch his breath. He hears the car tires screech towards him; he quickly starts running down the sidewalk heading into the street.

[GANG MEN IN CAR SPEEDING]

Lamar is terrified! He frantically approaches a nearby Intersection street. As soon as Lamar's foot reaches the middle of the Intersection, he disappears. His entire body ran through an invisible Portal to another Dimension.

Example photo

It appears to the gang members that Lamar vanished in the thin air right in front of them. The gang member's car comes to screeching halt. In disbelieve, both Gang men on foot stop, slowly approaching the intersection spot that Lamar disappears at.

CAR DRIVER; Did that nigga just disappear?
FRONT SEAT PASSENGER; Naaww. Hell naaww, he went around the corner.
BACK SEAT PASSENGER; "how the fuck could he go around the corner?
Car Driver; "well where the fuck did, he goes then?"

[Far Distance, PARKED CIA CAR-VAN]

Example photo

Parked White Company Radar Surveillance Van, Tinted windows. The windows are rolled down. Inside sits two white, middle-aged men, looking at the Gang car and foot chase through Binoculars. With CIA badge on the arm, they are spying to see if the Gang members carried out their assigned mission to Kill Lamar.

DRIVER OF CIA VAN; The Mission Has Been Compromised AGAIN.

[In slow motion, Aerial view of the Neighborhood Block]

Sky view of CIA white Van. Two Gang members confused bewildered continue walking in all directions. Gang car circles the area. Lamar is gone.

EXT. Promise Land. Night.

Lamar continues running, "Unaware" that he has entered in the "Promise Land." Frantic he stumbles as he runs up the stairs that lead him to, two huge Gold Double Doors. He rushes in falling on the floor in exhaustion, fear, and panic.

Three beautiful Black Galactic women [MALTA, NAGUS, and KAH] look down upon him standing over him, as Lamar lays on the floor on his back.

The three Galactic women look at Lamar in a caring, concerned way. Malta; He finally made it; she motions them to take Lamar upstairs. Exhausted, Lamar passes out.

[SCREEN SLOWLY FADES INTO BLACK]

Two 15ft Tall Black Galactic Men pick up Lamar's lifeless body and gently lays him down on this floating blue glowing hospital type bed. Floating Bed has no legs or wheels underneath it.

[Next Character Scene Story]

[ACTION]

EXT. Venice Beach California. Beachside Boardwalk. Hot Bright Sunny Evening.
[Music: The Last in Line, by Dio]

Overview; of Beach & Boardwalk Scene, many young and old, mainly white people, are mingling about along the boardwalk and beach.

Josh and his Skater buddies are skating in between the public. Weaving from side to side to avoid hitting anyone, skating their way towards their destination. People are walking their dog; running on the beach, playing Frisbee, Volleyball, Flying Kites, etc.

[End of the song slowly fades away]

JOSH and two SKATER BUDDIES finally come to a curb to sit by a Tree to smoke a joint. Skater buddy #2; hands Josh a joint and say's fire it up! Josh lights it up with his lighter and inhales the Marijuana.
JOSH; "you know, if my parents saw me smoking, they'd have a fucking fit!
SKATER #3; Laughs.
JOSH; I mean damn (Josh inhales holding his breath while talking) I'm 17 years old for Christ sake, what the hell do they expect, (Exhale the smoke) at least I still go to school, I'm not ah damn idiot I pay attention in class."
SKATER BUDDY #2; (laughs) fuck you dude, you do not pay attention for shit!"
SKATER BUDDY #3; Laughs.
JOSH; yes, the fuck I do pay attention. And how the hell would you know? We don't even have any classes together.
SKATER BUDDY #2; "DUDE" We have three freakin classes together!

[Flash Scene] High school, Reading classroom]
White Female Teacher, age 38, looks frustrated, impatient, standing at the chalkboard, slowly stops writing at the chalkboard because she realizes that JOSH is sleeping. JOSH is sitting at his desk sleeping while skater buddy #2 is leaning next to him shakes Josh to wake up.

[Flash Scene] Math Classroom]
White Female Teacher age 55, wearing classes, holding a clipboard looks frustrated, stands impatient tapping her foot, waiting for JOSH to wake up. Skater buddy #2 sitting next to Josh, shakes Josh, Muffled sounds of Skater buddy #2 wake up man, wake up!

[Flash scene] Chemistry classroom]
White male Teacher age 53, wearing a white lab coat, looks frustrated, stands impatient. Skater buddy #2 leans next to Josh, Muffled sound of skater buddy #2; Josh! Josh! Josh! is Asleep. Teacher slams the book on Josh's desk and Yells HEY!!

[EXT. Back at the Park Beach. Tree Curb side area.]

Josh nonchalantly rolling his eyes, looking guiltily, while smoking the joint.
JOSH; I don't, I don't remember ever seeing you there.
SKATER BUDDY #2; Sighs laugh while shaking his head.

[Across the Street.]
Two white male Venice Police Officers; is arresting an unknown white male.

JOSH: I can't understand what none of the Teachers is talking about. I can't sit there day after, day trying to learn something that has nothing to do with what I really want to do. What the fuck do Chemistry, TRIG or PE have to do with Architecture? I'm a "Hands on" kind of guy, you know? I like using my hands. Why don't they have Trade schools for people like me who simply want to get straight to the fucking point! I want to learn about Architecture, that's what I'm going to be an Architect Designer of Unique layouts.
Skate buddy #3; "Architect?"
JOSH; Yeah Architect of Theme Parks. Oh man, did you know my parents were talking about putting me in Juvenile."
Skater buddy #3; no-way man for what?
Skater buddy #2; yea man for what, that's fucking crazy.
JOSH; for fucking nothing! I'm telling you, man, these people are strict as HELL. can't do anything worth wild.
Skater Buddy #2; it's because you're adopted, that's the reason they're so strict.
Skater buddy #3; no fool, that isn't why there strict. No, there strict because their "Anal" You know, When, parents are always mad about something for nothing. That's being "Anal" Well, guess what? Your parents were Born that way."
JOSH; SHUT UP.

[Two white male Police Officers]
who arrest an unknown man earlier is approaching, walking across the street towards Josh and his skater buddies.
OFFICERS; you guys are not supposed to be here.
JOSH; Why not? We're not doing anything wrong, were sitting at the Park"
POLICE OFFICERS; Let me see some ID.
JOSH; ID? For what? What do you need to see my ID for?
POLICE OFFICERS; because I say so, now let me see some ID!!

JOSH; I don't have my ID on me. "sir" I'm at a Beach!
POLICE OFFICER; (angerly) stand up. GET ON YOUR FEET.
JOSH; WHAT THE FUCK DO YOU WANT? WHY ARE YOU HERE?
POLICE OFFICERS; grab Josh by his collar and starts punching him in the face, ribs, and stomach, continuing to tussle with Josh, banging Josh's head on the ground, blood comes out of his head, nose, and mouth.

SKATER BUDDY#2 and #3; What are you doing?!! Stop!! Leave him alone!!!

Josh is furiously beaten he is sent to the hospital with multiple fractures to his face, head, ribs, his face is unrecognizable, he is in critical condition.

Police Supervisor, the report notes Josh resisted arrested and threatened the Police with deadly force. Police Officers were never questioned or punished for the crime. One year later, soon after Josh, recovered the Police charged Josh with a Felony.

INT. California, Venice Courthouse. Morning.

Courthouse Characters; Josh, Police Officers, Judge, Plaintiff, Prosecuting Attorney, Audience, and Josh's Parents.

Court Police, wheels in Josh into the courtroom to await his sentencing for the false resisting arrest charged by the two Police Officers.

Josh sits in a wheelchair. He is disabled.

THE JUDGE; I Hereby sentence you to 2 years in Juvenile detention center.

Josh and his Parents are upset, grievance.

The Judge signs the Detention Center Papers. Suddenly the Judge sees the written order of the Detention Center Address change right before his eyes. The Judge takes off his glasses and rubs his eyes to get a clear look. The name of the Detention Center and the old Address Disappears. The Judge signs the orders to be approved for transporting Josh into the unknown facility.

JOSH; I don't deserve this, this is Bullshit!

Josh and other inmates board the detention center Van. Josh sits alone at the back seat on route to their destination. Josh Disappears. The van comes to a screeching halt. The driver turns completely around in his seat, unaware that Josh was collected into the Promise Land.

[Next Character Scene Story]

EXT. Los Angeles County California. Hot sunny day. Prison Yard, Folsom State Prison

KEITH, age 36, is outside on the prison yard lifting weights on a bench press; Two Black men stand on either side of Keith strikes up a friendly conversation as they SPOT Keith. We'll call these two inmates "THE SPOTTERS"

Inmate SPOTTER Description:

[Two Galactic Black Men, age looks around 30"s, Height 6'2, and the other one Height 5'9, from the Galactic Council of Seven, Planetary location; an area Nearby Sirius C] Their prison clothing is unusually "Pressed & Perfect" Their demeanor is calm and relaxed and when you're around them you feel very happy for no particular reason. They are there to bring the oppressed, impoverished suffering ones into the Promise Land. [Only certain people can see them]

Example photo

SPOTTER; So, what you in here for man, how much time you got in here?

KEITH is glad to explain he reflects what he did that brought him there and estimating how much time he was in prison.

INT. Keith's Apartment. Los Angeles California. Evening.

Both Keith and his girlfriend La-neesha arguing,
La-Neesha is nagging Keith because he's not bringing in enough money to pay the bills. Keith; "What the hell you think I'm doing? I am bringing in what I can! But, its hard LA-NEESHA nobody is hiring me for a job, and the ones that are hiring requires you to have ah Mutha fuckin high school diploma! And, I don't have that okay?! So, I have to sell this weed until I could stack up enough money to get us in a better neighborhood!!" The argument continues with La-neesha, (Sound is muffled.)

[In slow motion] The screen fades away into;
Keith gets on the phone calling his friends to come to pick him up.
Keith grabbing his coat and storms out of the apartment.

Keith is outside getting into the awaiting friend's car. His friends talk about robbing the corner store down the street. Keith tells them he's not robbing any store. They argue whether not they should rob the store. Keith is frustrated and orders the driver to pull over to let him out. Keith walks over to a nearby Bar. He spends an hour and 30 minutes inside.

EXT. Busy City Street. Late Night.

He leaves the Bar walking home. Two Police Officers with Guns drawn, orders Keith to get on the ground with his hands up. They arrest him for nothing "Claiming that Keith fits the description of a Corner Store Robbery. The three friends that Keith was riding in the car with were also arrested but, none of them did any Robbery. Instead of Robbing the Corner Store, they pulled up in front of one their Grand-mothers house to get some food and to bring it back to the sitting parked car to smoke some weed.

[NARRATED VOICE BY KEITH]
You see, we didn't realize that we were all being surveillance by a White CIA Company Radar Van with tinted windows. The Van is designed to pick up clear Audio sound inside of Cars, Building, and Homes to record everything that's being said. The CIA believes they have enough evidence to falsely accuse us of Robbing that store. They send out the Police to arrest us because, well, you already know that the Prison and Jail system is Big Business! The State Government makes over $50,000 dollars pre-housing Arrest. None of the arresting Police Officers nor the CIA men sitting in the Surveillance Van ever met me or my silly ass friends. Nor do they live in

my City Neighborhood. And, yet their Job is to create Mayhem, to Spy and to make false arrest in sending the unsuspecting Victims to Prison. That's right my friends make no mistake about it. This is "Government Corruption in its Finest Form!

EXT.
[Back at the Prison Yard]

Spotter; Keith meet me at that "TV Room Area" were having a meeting there, where we'll show you and other inmates how to escape from this place. To become one of the greatest people on earth and the most powerful too.
Keith; (Laughs) Yeah right man whatever, I'll be there.

Keith, the two spotters, and about thirty other inmates gather around to listen to one of the Spotters tell a Story.
One of the Spotter says; What if I told you that you can escape from this place right now without alarming one Guard.
Keith; I'll say you lost ya mind.
Spotter; What if I told you that "ALL Things are Possible"
Keith; Aww man here we go with that Jesus Religion Bullshit.
Spotters; Nope, what I'm about to say has nothing to do with Religion whatsoever. It's about knowing "Where You Are at" in this world and knowing Who You Are" Within the Containment of your Body. Just image yourself walking right out of here, just by walking through that wall over there. The moment you touch the wall you will see what's on the other side. And, what's on the other side is something EXTRAORDINARY. Beyond your WILDEST Imagination.

[As the Spotter describes the other side, the picture is revealed]
The most Beauty outdoor landscape with fruit trees, waterfalls, beautiful exotic animals, rolling green hillsides everywhere. Incredible Gold Pyramids Temples, as you walk you hear beautiful music, you walk further and hear laughter, you keep going a little further and see the most beautiful women in the world. And the most beautiful men in the world. "No homo though I'm just saying" that the world I'm talking about can't be described in words. You look around and notice it's the biggest Paradise land ever imagine, with a huge gold and silver crystal buildings and unique cars that fly. But you realize those aren't cars at all but different shaped floating houses! And you notice that the whole entire atmosphere Adores You, where you

truly feel Loved for no reason. And all you have to do is walk over to that wall and your already there. Go ahead try it"

Keith; Man, if only that was true though.
Spotter; Oh, but it is true, walk over to the wall and see.
Keith; Yeah that's a nice story but I'm going back to my Bunk.
INMATE; walks over to the wall and says, see, you can't go through. [Inmate falls through the wall on the other side] He instantly disappears. The rest of the Inmates are Shocked. Saying where did he go?
Spotters; He went on the other side.

The Spotter walks over to the wall placing one arm through the wall to show the inmates what's possible. All the inmates walk over to the wall. The inmates start to place their hands through the wall. The inmates standing behind the front row start to push and shove their way into the wall while looking back to see if the Guards can see them.

Example photo

Not realizing that all of them were already on the other side the moment the spotter said, "Meet me in the TV Room Area" The Dimension portal is the TV area. And, not the Wall. When either one of the spotters tells an inmate to meet them in the TV Room Area. They instantly disappear the moment they walk in the TV Area. But to the inmate, they believe they are sitting in the chair gather into the TV room.

Because in their minds they're still in prison. But, to remove themselves from the mental state of being in Prison. The Spotters must tell them a story of using their imagination on how to get to the other side. The guards and certain inmates cannot see the Spotters. The Guards have no recollection of any inmate disappearing as if the inmate who went on the other side never came to that prison facility. When an inmate comes to a Guard with concerns of their missing inmate friend. The guards suggest that they get some Counseling for seeing a made-up imaginary person. There are two Spotters in every Prison throughout America. And, the Prisoners are disappearing in record numbers. Keith and other inmates will be changed into powerful Human beings to return to help others overcome hardship, depression, poverty, mental enslavement, and Government Corruption.

[Next Character Scene Story]

[The Introduction of Victoria's Arrival]
[Ominous Sound Music]

TRAGIC SCENE FLASHES 1966-1968 Civil Rights Area.
A series of Flash scenes; of black men and women hanging on trees. Tulsa Oklahoma Black Wall Street burning to the ground. Churches being burned to the ground. Medgar Everest; Standing on Stage, then him laying in the Driveway. Malcolm X; Standing on Stage, then a flash scene of him Laying in the Coffin. JFK; Standing on Stage, then a flash scene of him being shot. The Black Panthers; Is feeding hungry School Children and giving a speech to black victims of extreme oppression. Then flash scene of the Black Panthers being shot down by Police as they slept in their beds, the scene is shown 4 other Black Panthers being unfairly imprisoned for life.
 [The Voice of Dr. Martin Luther King giving the Promise Land speech]

EXT. Memphis. Lorraine Motel. Day.

April 4th, 1968 Dr. Martin Luther King is shown standing on the balcony of the Lorraine Motel with five other men. [Two Black men are shown standing next to Dr. King. They are the CIA culprits in the assassination plot of Dr. King- Sinister Look and slow-motion movement that is displayed in their mannerisms] Suddenly a SHOT REIGN OUT [White male Sheriff, holding a Riffle leaps over a wall directly across from the Lorraine Motel and jumps into an awaiting Sheriff Patrol Vehicle] Hitting Dr. King in the neck on the balcony; he falls on the floor.

INT. Memphis Hospital.

[In slow motion] Dr. King is then being wheeled into the emergency room hospital the Doctor is standing to wait for Dr. King to come into the operating room Dr. King is still alive his eyes are open and is alert. Dr. King is brought into the room, three other white FBI male agents come into the operating room, and the Nurse is ordered to leave the room. The Nurse comes out and immediately turns back to look at what's happening, the nurse sees all three FBI agents spitting on Dr. King's face then slowly cover his face with a Pillow, the sound of struggle follows, then the heart mummer indicts no longer breathing. *(Based on the Book "The Assassination Plot to Kill King" Written by Dr. King's Attorney Dr. William Pepper)*

Dr. King Spirit/Soul is now floating above the hospital room, outside and above the neighborhood-City, Dr. King's Soul/Spirit travels in the air and stops at his brother house where he sees him being attacked and murdered by government agents. King Soul travels to a church where his mother is being shot in the face, he then travels right above where a baby girl is being born.

[NARRERATED Male Voice]

INT. Hospital: April 10, 1968, Time 8:16 Pm Chicago ILL,
A beautiful baby girl is born, and she has very Powerful beings looking after her.
[Three glowing female human forms Floating above Victoria]
At the age of five Victoria, mental comprehension is more advanced than others around her. She is aware that very Powerful Beings somehow brought her Soul down to earth. At an early age, she is concerned for the people of earth. And, thinks to herself. If the Spirit of evil and darkness is not contained properly? It will prevent the balance of "Good," to flow abundantly with the people. This will stifle the world forever. She is then Compelled to pray to this "Unknown Powerful Source" to grant her the ability to bring down the Promise Land. Her Elementary school teachers overheard young Victoria telling a story about the Promise Land. she was then sent to the Guidance counsel which led Victoria to be sent to another school for mentally disturbed Children. Since then Victoria has Suppressed the information about the Promise Land. Many years have passed until this one afternoon on April 10, 2020, in Los Angeles changed everything.

Victoria, age 29, has two small children, she is gripped by poverty. She escapes her abusive relationship. With no money and nowhere to go she sought refuge at a Skid Row Homeless shelter. She waves goodbye at the corner to send her children off to school. Walking down a busy sidewalk street headed back to her shelter. She sees a crowd gathering of about 60 Black and White people. Through the crowds of people, she sees a homeless man wearing dark torn tattered clothing speaking passionately to the crowd. Something like a Master Teacher of Wisdom and Knowledge is Captivating.

[HOMELESS MAN SPEAKS]

Pitch: Actor Orlando Jones [Anansi, the Storyteller on American Gods]

"What is the use of a "God" who only dwells in Heaven?"

It appears we may be the lost Gods or Demi-Gods who are blindly walking around in this Hellish earth. All we have to do is look around, and see how our place in time ended up being so dysfunctional? We'll begin to see just how the so-called "African Americans" or should I say the "Indigenous Negro Americans" What? GO LOOK IT UP...But how did we end up living in such a Backwards and Upside- down society?" Whereas, the Indigenous Negro's are the ones who created Advanced civilizations throughout America. And yet, how did we "Really" end up at such a low point of existence? How on Earth did we end up asking for help from the oppressor? Where the very people who founded this Country are now the same people paying thousand upon millions of dollars for their own Land?

Think about that...We are Indigenous to our own land and yet we could all end up in prison by the hands of a FOREIGNER. Throughout history, we were "Supposed to believe that we were concorded and enslaved by a small group of primitive knuckle dragging Europeans from the Caucus Mountains of Hell-sinki Russia.

The question is. How could they suddenly have the skills and Power to take over the most Powerful people on the Planet? An Ancient People that's been around for MILLION of Years... HOW?

Now... what I'm about to tell you, is way beyond your imagination. Hold on to your hats because most of you could not even conceive of this truth. I'll tell you how the white man evolved so quickly. They received some help. [Sinister laugh] Oooh, but not just by anybody. No, the Europeans received some Help from something that is NOT HUMAN.

[Crowd Mumbles]

Well, how do you explain their evolution process? They were Grunting, Walking on all Fours in Caves as the Neanderthal Blood runs through their veins Today. And to suddenly walk upright carrying nooses and shotgun Rifles? How do you explain the Ancient UFO Portraits that are painted by Leonardo Davinci, the Roman Catholic, and Germans?

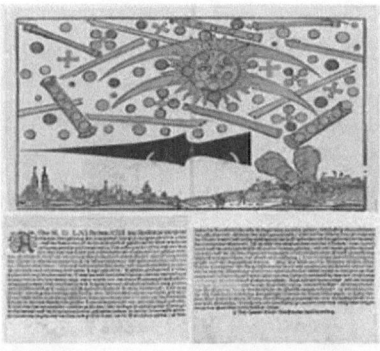

What? You think they just woke up one day and decided to draw some UFO'S?

Christopher Columbus. Wrote in his Journal that he was guided by a strange round Disk-Shaped Bright Light in the Sea and in the sky that leads him to America's. And, yet "They" KNEW HE WAS A SAVAGE. But they led him here, anyway didn't they? Yes "They" did these Muthafuckas...

That right makes no mistake about it something outside of our Intelligence has orchestrated their entire lives to take- over America and this world.

In the year 1619 "These... "Beings" orchestrated the Slaughter of the Indigenous Negro elders and most of the Parents. For the purpose of their bloodline descendants to take advantage, to take possession, to oppress, enslave and Brainwash the Young for 400 years. And, now here it Is 2019, blood drunk from their own greed and power with the help of their military protection. But of course, there's always a Beginning and an End to all things. And according to the Congress Archives slavery started in 1619. And, the Bible said slavery would last 400. And what do you know? Its 400 Years...

They would naturally assume that their Reign would end by the hands of the Oppressed people. But oh they're wrong... No, these "Beings" are far clever than that. Their reign will end by the hands of their own. Well, look around you right now. They are at WAR with THEMSELVES.

[In Office Fight Scene-Democrats vs Republicans]

Their criminal Laws that are woven throughout the fabric of our society was designed to keep black people under severe oppression and in a state of permanent poverty. Ultimately it constituted our living environment as Hell on Earth. This whole set up was deliberately done to us on PURPOSE. Otherwise, our existence to this earth would not make any sense. Maybe our purpose on earth is to "Prefect our Souls" through pain and anguish. Like a Diamond in the ruff. Or was this all done to us in Vain? I mean, after all, you don't think the "Creators, did all this "Hard Work on us for nothing? [Sinister Grin} I think not... Judgment is coming to my Friends...This Human Masquerade will all soon come to an Abrupt and Shocking End."

[The Homeless Man stares directly at Victoria]

Suddenly, the wind, trees, and leaves begin to blow, increasing its force the homeless crowd disperses. As Victoria walks away, she notices someone standing in the middle of the street not affected by the guts of wind, debris or cars driving by. It's a Black woman dressed in Sleek Futuristic Jumpsuit, with something small flying around her head. Victoria takes a closer look. It's a tiny person the size of a small cell phone floating gently onto the woman's shoulder. They both look at Victoria with concern and yet caring feeling to her. Victoria is utterly shocked and amazed; she suddenly sees a flashback of her childhood being visited by 3 Galactic Female Beings.

[Vision of the Promise Land downloaded into Victoria's mind],

Galactic Women Being is showing her places of great Beauty and Magic, in a Prosperous, Happy Free Environment of Enlightenment. A voice enters Victoria's mind. MALTA; Very soon you will bring the "Promise Land" to

America. The Promise Land is a world created within the Galaxy located on "Sirius C" this Energy" must come down to Planet Earth soon. Allowing a dimensional portal to secretly establish itself within most inner cities throughout America. You will help Millions into the Promise Land.

[Flash scene of Lamar, Josh, and Keith]

Those individuals will assist you throughout your Journey, they too will be completely changed, having some of the greatest powers in the world. They will then return to help others overcome Oppression, Hardship, Mental enslavement, and Government Tyranny.

Victoria is suddenly jolted and snaps back into reality shaken by a HOMELESS WOMEN; is nudging her with a Bible saying "Are you alright? Honey are you Okay?" Victoria looks at the homeless women and then looks at where the Galactic Female was standing. The Galactic Being" is gone. The Homeless women say, "Were all getting ready for Church Bible study wanna come? All your answers are in the Good Book. Victoria is still in shock she completely ignores the homeless women and calmly walks away in disbelief.

Meanwhile, in Washington D.C. the U.S. Government is preparing for "Otherworldly" hostile forces that are entering Earth's Atmosphere.

INT. Nuremberg Germany United Nations Building- Secret Meeting. Midnight.

A Secret Emergency Meeting in Nearby Switzerland between the ISG-International Shadow Government, NASA, the Vatican, and the U.S. Councils; Folks, something Otherworldly is headed this WAY.
NASA STAFF; Why? Why are "They" coming now?
[ISG STAFF, recalls in their mind of the reason "They" are Arriving]

INT. Galactic Meeting Hall. Time on Earth, the Year 1119 A.D.
Planetary Location; Planet Saturn and Sirius C.

A meeting conducted by the Galactic High Council and the Council of Seven. They are the "Overseers" within our Solar System. They are also the bloodline Relatives of Black people and "Certain" White People on Earth.

[The Galactic High Council Lecture Speaks]

Some of you may be aware that a meeting took place between our Alliance and the Evil (Galactic) "Tak-con" known as the Tak-conians." We discussed and decided that the "Land Treaty" would be held by the Tak-cons" since their Planet is now but all destroyed. They will live in Certain parts of Earth Solar System. We agreed that their colonization would be for 400 years on Earth. Suddenly, the Council of Seven Congregation is in an uproar. They are enraged by the High Council's decision. They demanded that Tak-cons be placed in shackles and removed from the Solar System at ONCE.

The Galactic High Council Speaks; Now Calm down, this is only "Temporary" I can assure you all, that we will be monitoring everything that goes on so that nothing gets out of hand. And that the people of Earth will not be harmed nor be aware that this is going to happen. They cannot and will NOT be destroyed by the arrival and migration of the "Tak-conians." The Earth's Moon will be used as our Surveillance and Calendar count down set on Earth Year 1519 the day that the Tak-cons reign ends on Earth.

Restless by the decision of the High Council, the Council of Seven unleash the deadliest Plague on Europe in 1310-1347 in the attempt to remove Tak-cons bloodline from Earth. [The Tak-cons will later use that footage against the Council of Seven]

[Earth, the Year 1519] The celebration begins in the Galaxy for the end of the Tak-conians reign. One of the Council of Seven noticed a strange glitch in the moon's radar surveillance system. While all others are in celebration. Two of the Council of Seven have uncovered something strange. They quickly strip away the full imagery, and to their Horror, they discovered that the actual Year on Earth is 2020 and not 1519!

Horrified they discover that the people of Earth have been in bondage and misery for an additional 500 years! The evil Tak-conians Kept the people of Earth under a perpetual reincarnation of Tyranny and Destruction. They used a highly advanced Holographic imaging system that shows a reenactment of the Tak-cons bloodline falling from their reign by using the Plague 1310-1347" and a fake attack above Europe in 1547. And

Secretly hides the location of Earth adding additional years to their reign that was set for 1000 years.

They also discovered the U.S. Government is fully aware of the Moon Calendar count down" due to being in Close Contact with the Tak-cons. This is considered the most heinous crimes ever committed in the Galaxy. Known as the "C.M.R-Controversial Moon Revelation"

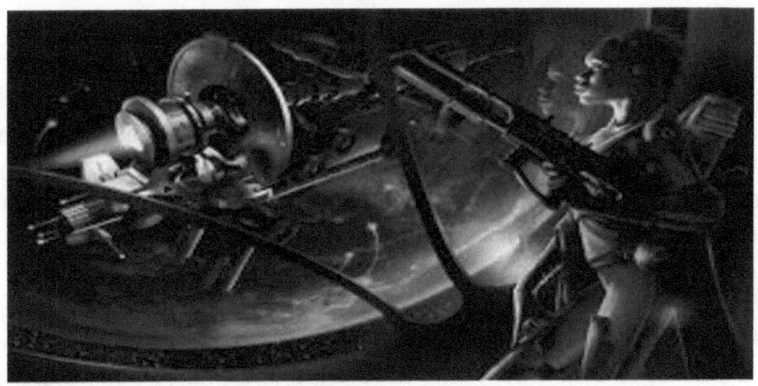

[Galactic Battle between Good and Evil]

Two of the Council of Seven takes the "C.M.R." from the dark side of the Moon to give to the High Council, but they are being watched by the evil Tak-conians who will stop at nothing to keep the secret hidden. Fighting begins between the two factions.

The 5 of the Council of Seven is killed in the process. The evil Tak-cons take the victims ship and their bodies to the incinerator. Another group of evil Tak-cons who were there during the killings suddenly noticed a cloaked ship of one of the Council of Seven in their radar.

Inside the Cloaked ship sits three crying females who witnessed the whole thing. Its MALTA, NAGUS, and KAH. With their ship's ability to record everything they now have the "Secret C.M.R." saddened by the people of Earth who suffered for so long they become enraged, attempting to inform the others. Suddenly their ship is hit with a powerful beam by the Tak-cons. Knocking out all communications.

The Tak-cons cannot allow the Council of Seven to go to the High Council. MALTA, NAGUS, and KAH embark on a heroic effort to save the people of earth. They rush down to earth with their ship to give Victoria the Ancient Secret Power Plasma. Victoria and millions of others are unaware of what's going on, but they suddenly feel something being, download into their subconscious mind. It's the Ancient DNA Plasma if combined with their sadness of unfortunate situations of living through Government Tyranny, is the unveiling Key to the Universe which will transform Victoria and millions into one of the most Powerful Beings.

"Malta" secretly cloak Victoria from any Galactic Evil from seeing her. In their efforts to download the Promise Land Portal Implementations and the C.M.R. into Victoria's mind. That would give her the Power to transform into the most Powerful Superbeing on Earth. The United States Government and its Military is informed by the Evil Tak-cons and they prepare for the worst. The Tak-conians are allies, and together they feed off the negative energy from the people of earth of any Race, Creed or Nationality. They can only exist in a world with War, Bloodshed, Suffering, and Destruction. They have restrained and murdered many in the past who tried to provide evidence of the C.M.R. So; this leads them in hot pursuit of the one who holds the Key to it all. Desperate, to stop the one who can end their reign they unleash a deadly virus into America's Urban core, buses, Airports, etc. Many are dying. Victoria Chakras system is triggered by approaching deadly danger this automatically changes her into one of the most Powerful.

The Promise Land magically appears right through her Chakra system. Victoria then flies to various parts of the Inner-cities and unleashes the Portals that open and lead to the Promise Land. Victoria thinks about her friends that have suffered and died in the past. She goes back 10 years where she was able to lead her suffering friend into the Promise Land. She then thinks of the ATLANTIC SLAVE TRADE. And, goes back 400 years unleashing the Promise Land throughout America. And, finds out that most enslaved people can't even conceive of the Promise Land. Therefore, it doesn't exist for those who can't conceive of it Those who are ready to see it, will see it. Victoria fast forwards herself back to 2020 And is met up with Lamar, Josh, and Keith together, they work as mentors for the Inner cities to open the eyes and the mind of those who are mentally trapped.

Together they open up bright doorway pathways, as they open up the people are shocked amazing to suddenly being enthralled by the most extraordinary Neighborhood Transformation ever recorded. The most Beautiful Structural Landscape forming right before their eyes! Like out of a dream but this is no dream. This is Reality, suddenly appear the most amazing Theme Park & Housing Community Combined forming all around the area. They can't move their so mesmerized the people of the Inner cities are amazed as they stand they're pinching themselves to make sure they're not dreaming. The wind starts to blow a bright blue color. The blue wind blows gently through their body as it is dancing in and around their face.

They gradually breathe in this soft Blue Wind. As it tickles their nose, they are suddenly jolted as it transforms their "Thinking" they breath in Higher Consciousness. Billion-year-old Ancient Identity of the past they suddenly remember. They are breathing in great Wisdom and Powerful Magic elements. Their eyes, face, and body begin to change transforming into a better version of themselves. They appear much healthier with better-looking bodies and their presence is of Love, Power, Respect, Wisdom, and Compassion.

Their tone is very calm and pleasant to be around, and they have a great sense of humor. They now have the intelligence to successfully govern their own State and Country. Their Charka system has infinite power so great they could pull out various Silly and Powerful Creatures at Will. Creatures and Animals of all sizes, forms, shapes, and colors. The People are transforming and now they can heal, talk telepathically, Posses Great Telekinesis skills, they can fly, float, walk through walls, disappear reappear they travel in Spaceship of various styles and shapes. They know now that their mission is to make sure the American people of all Races are not being victimized by government corruption, tyranny or evil individuals Their specialty beside hosting Block Parties in their wonderous land of S.S.H.E.A. is to open the eyes of the mentally enslaved, save people from severe negativity and become a guardian to those who are in need. They are none other than S.S.S.H;

"THE SUCCESSFUL SERVICE SUPERHEROES".

The Successful Service Superheroes were once Victims of government corruption, Civil Rights Leaders, Visionaries, Teachers, Mentors, X Gang members, Drug dealers, Prostitutes, Drug addicts, Teen Run always, Impoverished individuals, Abused Foster Children and Teens, Juveniles, Incarcerated individuals, homeless families, individuals with Depression. They are transformed into the most powerful Superheroes!

Evil no longer has ANY effect on the Successful Service Superheroes. And MALTA, NAGUS, and KAH along with the entire Universe are extremely Happy! A real celebration takes place. Millions of people finally have their unique abilities to take control of their own lives once and for all!

Victoria, Lamar, Josh, and Keith changes thousands of impoverished rundown abandoned Neighborhoods all over America. Into Places of Great Beauty, Prosperity Wonderment and Enlightenment. They can only be seen by the oppressed one, the impoverished one, the wise one and Chosen one of "ANY" Color, Race or Nationality. The Promise Land is completely **Invisible** to Individuals that are Unconscious, Evil and Ignorant.

[The Closing of the Movie]

Victoria is at a public Zoo disguised as the Zookeeper. She opens the cage with her Telekinesis skills of an imprisoned Gorilla; the Gorilla holds out his hand and Victoria gently walk him out of his cage. As they walk along the pathway

Victoria: "So...You like Grapes?"

[Music is heard]

The entire Zoo landscape all Animals cages are opening, the Animals, Birds, Creatures, and Critters are following Victoria and the Gorilla. As she leads them to the Promise Land. Victoria has a Bright Golden Glow shining throughout her Clothing. Then the entire town is shown with people who are like Victoria (The Powerful Superheroes) of having a bright golden glow around them as well. They are leading other people out of their unfortunate condition towards the Promised Land. Then the camera shows short clips of various States across America, then throughout Africa, South America, Cambodia, People who have the Bright Glow leading people to the Promised Land. It is still evil on earth but, this time, Good and Evil are on an even playing field. Earth is now a world of Superheroes and Villains alike.

The End

I hope you enjoyed the Dramatic Sci-fi Film Treatment
of The Arrival of the Promise Land.

Problem Statement #1

Problem Statement #1

Since the time of Slavery, Jim Crow era. Homes, churches, Prominent thriving successful black businesses, and communities would often be destroyed by "Certain" racist individuals throughout the occupied 13 colonies. These groups would often become enraged of the very thought of successful black business owners thriving and expanding throughout the surrounding areas. Such as the success of a black community in Tulsa Oklahoma called "Black Wall Street." It was one of the largest black successful communities in America. And, in 1921 all businesses, churches, and homes were set on fire, bombed and destroyed by a white racist terrorist group called the (KKK) Ku Klux Klan and/or {Government Organized Crime Groups}.

These KKK groups wore hooded garments to cover their head and face. To hide their identity from their neighborhood citizens particularly Black Americans. That wouldn't be able to identify the perpetrators as ordinary working citizens. Such as members of the top CIA, FBI, Police Departments, Court Judges, Attorney's, U.S. Congress, Planned Parenthood, CDC, Federal Drug & Vaccine Commission and U.S. Senate, Food and Drug, Federal Reserve Systems, etc.

All these Unwarranted Service Groups systemically destroy the livelihood and wellbeing of all Indigenous Negro Americans and African Americans way of life. Here is a brief list of a Black community destroyed by deliberate systematic genocide:

- A well-established organization in Oakland California called "The Black Panthers" founded in 1966 by Ph.D. The University of California, Huey P. Newton and Bobby Seale student of Politics and Engineering. Their organization was designed to protect Indigenous communities from any kind of Police brutality and Government Corruption. The Black Panthers were the first organized group in Oakland California to start the "Free Breakfast and Lunch School Program. The head of the "FBI" J Edgar Hoover destroyed the successful organization by murdering most of the group and one of the Leaders and his wife was murdered in their Bed. Then the FBI illegally arrested the rest sending them to prison for life.
- Dr. Martin Luther King, his Brother, and his Mother were assassinated. Dr. King went on a Poor Persons Campaign. Also scheduled to meet with the U.S. Congress regarding "Reparations" for the Indigenous Negros. He never made it to that meeting. They later found the CIA and FBI was involved in the murder. And, in 1999 the Justice Supreme Court, Jury found the U.S. Government **Guilty!** Of the Wrongful Death of Dr. King.
- Soon after the murders of Civil Rights Leaders; The Honorable Malcolm X, Medgar Everest, The Black Panthers, Dr. Khali Muhammad. All prominently black communities across America

were suddenly flooded with the most dangerous and addictive drug narcotics in the world. During 1968- 1994- 2016 Top FBI and CIA informant "drug smuggler Barry Seal, Governor at the time Bill Clinton and his Brother Roger Clinton received the okay from President Ronald Regan to smuggle tons of pure cocaine directly into the Indigenous Negro Communities this smuggling ring operation is still going on today. For the fact, that has never been any Opium nor Cocaine fields ever grown in America. And yet they seem to always find its way into American homes.

- Then when the communities were completely saturated. Ronald Reagan creates a campaign slogan of "Just Say No to Drugs" using the media and TV Commercials as a sales pitch to create "War on Drugs" Tactics that were meant for "War against the Indigenous Negro Americans and African Americans". This created an excuse for the U.S Government to train the Police in an all-out racist Man Hunt to viciously beat, murder and lock up anyone who had this overseas, overflown drug in their possession. Sending millions of Indigenous men and women to prison. Another tactic used to entrap victims into a modern-day style slave system. Was to arrest and imprisoning anyone with Marijuana possession. Knowing full well that Marijuana is a Natural Healing Medicine that have not killed one person. And yet, Cigarettes are Government man-made approved and has killed well over 4-Million people within a course of 30 years. Moreover, their full funded and most profited Pharmaceutical companies and the demand for their HHS Vaccine shots is the leading cause of Retardation and Autism. Represented and manufactured by the U.S. Government Business Corporation.

This is Public Information Provided by the Victim themselves. If you want to learn more about the FBI-CIA involvement 1969-1984-2016 of the drug smuggling ring. Simply Google or YouTube, Top CIA Informant the late Barry Seal/ Senior Bush/Bill Clinton.

In the Honorable Great, Dr. Martin Luther King own words of the Indigenous Negros being exposed to Congress Assembled Corruption and Abuse.

The Great Dr. Martin Luther King Speech regarding "We Were Here"

"Much of America strays from the ideals of Justice goals of America, is Freedom…Used and Scorned though we may be. Our destiny is tied up in the destiny of America. Before the Pilgrims foraged this land to Plymouth. "We Were Here" Before Jefferson etched across the pages of history the majestic words of the declaration of independence. "We Were Here" Before the words of the star-spangled banner were written. "We Were Here" For more then 2-Centuries our forbearers labor here without any wages. They made Cotton King" they built the homes of their Foreign Oppressors during the most humiliating and oppressive Conditions. And out of a Bottomless Vitality! They continued to grow and develop. One hundred years later, the negro is still languishing in the corners of American society and finds himself an Exile in his own Land."

Dr. Martin Luther King Regarding: "Promissory Note for the People"

"So, we have come here today to dramatize a shameful condition. In a sense we have come to the Nation Capitol to "Cash a Check" When the architects of the Republic wrote the Constitution and the Declaration of Independence they were signing a "Promissory Note" to which every American was to "Fall Heir too" This "Note" was a "Promise" that ALL Men, YES, Black Men as well as White Men. Would be guaranteed the unalienable Rights of Life, Liberty, and the Pursuit of Happiness."

Dr. King discovered Congress's fraud and corruption in their Financial & Land assistance Programs

In Dr. King's own words: *"At the very same time that America "Congress" refused to give the negroes any "Land" Through an act of "Congress" the U.S. government was giving away Millions! of Acres of Land in the West and in the mid-West, which meant that it was willing to undergird its white peasants from Europe with Economic floor, but not only did they give the land. They built land grant Colleges. With government money to teach them how to farm. Not only that, they provided County agents to further their expertise in farming. Not only that, they provided low interest's rates in order that they mechanize their farms, not only that today many of these people are receiving Millions! in federal subsidy not to farm. And they are the very people telling the Black Man that he outta "Lift Himself Up by His Own Boot Straps"...And this is what we are faced with, and this a reality... Now when we come to Washington in this Campaign, we're coming to get our Check"*

"Dr. MARTIN LUTHER KING JR."

This public information was found at my local Library and Online Google

"Indeed, to Allow "Any" Race of people to rule the world will eventually be the Death of the World itself."

Let's Analyze Occurrences That's Out of this World

What if the atrocities that were just outlined were contributed to Otherworldly or Extraterrestrial influences and involvement? Now I know that sounds 100% crazy. But, for over 30 Years I experienced, studied and Researched Human History and UFO/Alien agenda. This subject matter will never be taught in schools, you must experience it for yourself. Through extensive research based on perspective common sense and all logical reasoning. We can safely say that 1 out of 10 people have seen or had an encounter with a Spaceship or Alien. Whether anyone wants to admit it or not is irrelevant. What matters is that we recognize the overall scope of how our world has drastically changed through "Otherworldly" influences. Our way of life has changed from once a civilization that thrived under simplicity and the natural order of things that were Good. Into a world that is completely Evil, Backwards and Dysfunctional. When we look at how times have changed over the past 17th Century till this very day. We can say there has been some sort of "Otherworldly Intervention" that have shaped the way we live our lives. For example; we have gone from the Horse-drawn carriage and buggy to the Advance self-driving Cars and Airplanes. From Ancient Scrolls, 1600's Postcards- News Papers. To Satellite Television, Cell Phones, and Computers. Where is this advanced technology coming from?

And, please. Don't consider the notion of Charles Darwin Evolution theory. When we all know his entire Bloodline was the last Human creation on Earth. Every other race already had advanced Civilizations thousands of years prior to his genetic existence. Darwin's entire work was based on a "Theory".

Here's what's been proven; the further back we go in history the more Advance we really are. Try and wrap your mind around this notion; we are so advanced in our Evolution that a group of "Alien Beings or People" (however you wish to call them) have invented a technology that literally Placed the Entire World in a time continuum of Re-incarnation of the past. That's right we are NOT living in the Present" day and time as most of us believe. No, we are living in the past. If they brought us to our Present time, we would be 2 Billion years ahead of this time. One great example: Consider the fact 1 out of 10 people have seen or was involved in UFO contact. So, the question is "How did "Time" skip over us about the knowledge of these Spaceships? Why do "They" have the ability to travel in and out of Dimension and Time? While most people on earth can't even conceive of this? "Why" did Earth become excluded from the "Advanced Information" that everyone in the galaxy seems to already have? Why are we "Placed Back in Time" left with the primitive Automobiles and Airplanes?

Some people believe that when the Earth was made, people automatically started popping up out of Nature Gardens. Referenced to the "Story" of the Bible. Where it speaks of the Man who magically appears in the Garden and takes part of his rib to create the Woman. But of course, that is not how human creation works. The Honorable Historian and researcher of Metaphysics Mr. Bobby Hemmitt speak about how we were all brought here from other Primal worlds other than earth. The Dogon Tribe in Africa speaks of their race coming from Planet Sirius B. As well as the Egyptians in which their Pyramids are aligned in the direction of Orion's Belt. The Ancient Ethiopians texts teach that they originated from Planet Saturn and Mars. Way before NASA ever knew of the Planet existence. And speaking of NASA. A scientist from NASA, NACA, AMES named Dr. Norman Bergrum wrote the book "The Ring Makers of Saturn" and another Scientist Engineer for the Apollo Space Stations Mr. Clark McClelland wrote a book called "Stargate Chronicles"

Both NASA Scientist explains on a YouTube interview in 2014 that our Universe is incredibly advanced, and it is being operated by Pre-dominantly of the "Black Race" and by several different Creatures. And that the Earth was made for the Black Race. Dr. Bergrum Authored a Book entitled "The Ring Makers of Saturn" in that book he shows pictures of the Rings around Saturn being made by a huge Spaceship. With its Plasma fuel flying around Saturn, three times the Size of Earth. Dr. Bergrum's Space Satellite recorded two very tall Black Males coming off their Plasma ship. They came to help fix a problem that was related to the U.S. Satellite and Shuttle. They told the U.S. Men that they are the Makers of the Rings Around Saturn" what disturbs Dr. Bergrums the most is that they are making more Rings around other Planets as well. In which he's assuming that Earth is next. As he put it in one of his interviews "Things are getting Critical"

Now I know what you're thinking. You're saying to yourself. "Oh my god, this is the most ridiculous stuff I ever read"

Yes, I Understand, really, I do... That's why it's good to read this book as "Entertainment Purposes only" Because our human life is greater than any

"Fiction story" ever written. So, hold on to your seats because you're in for one Hell-of-a Ride. This book is also for people who are "Unaware" of Certain important things and Events that they Should be Aware of" There are certain subjects that the Media, Films, and the school systems never really talk about. And yet it's one of the most important issues in the world for all races, colors, and cultures. So, the moral portion of this chapter is;

Not only are we being influenced by "Otherworldly Beings" but part of the influences is Evil and are from the dark side or the lower level of Dimensions. whereas these humans who are made by these evil entities are made without Souls. These are the most dangerous Beings in the Universe known for destroying their own Planet prior to coming here. They only want to cause destruction and tyranny on worlds because that's how they feed themselves.

This evil influence thrives from the "Innocent Unsuspecting People" who hold tremendous edible energy through their Chakras. They hate anything that is Good and often times they hover around a person for days or years causing the person to have Depression or Mental Illness. The Indigenous people of Earth has an abundance of healthy energy. That has been corrupted in the past 300 years. Many are being consumed by this evil influence. And it's very important to pinpoint exactly what kind of people are under a greater galactic evil influence. Once we see "Who's Who" in this world, we will begin to know what their next planned agenda is and how to avoid it. While we attempt to implement the Promise Land Communities throughout America.

So, first, let's explore a bit of History first to understand what "Bloodline" is more likely to be influenced by outside evil forces than other races. Not to discriminate, place blame, stereotyping or to be negative. NO! That is NOT what this portion of the book is about. It's to educate those who are unaware of what they genetically attract within themselves. And, for the sake of all humanity should never hold any position of power except in their own home.

<u>So, without Further Ado:</u>

The Introduction: Historical Origin and Way of life of Humanity

Imagine for a moment in this true to the life situation of an American Horror Tragedy. Imagine, that a group of Psychopathic Serial Killers broke into your home (Country) and murdered half of your family members (People Population). And then used the resources from your home (Lands, Natural Resources, Valuable Possessions) to establish their unwarranted government business corporation. A made-up government system that Goes Against the Grain of All Humanity. Designed to not only dictate to "YOU" on how you should live your life. But, have illegally set up their system (U.S. government Business Corporation) to destroy your very Livelihood, destroy your identity, to keep "You" and everyone that "You" know in a perpetual state of poverty, despair and misery. And, now as a result of the Foreign invasion of your home. You're now struggling to put food on the table, you don't even own the home that you're living in or the Land that you are standing on. Now the foreign invaders own everything that is inherited to you. You can't even get land to plant a garden without paying thousands of dollars for it. (Being forced to pay for your own Land) This is how government Corruption and Tyranny is woven in the fabric of our Society today. And it's the #1 cause of Poverty, Homelessness, Crime, and Depression.

According to Any "New World Dictionary of American English.

<u>Definition of Indigenous</u>: 1 existing or produced naturally in a region or Country; belonging (to) as a native two innate; inherent; inborn; Indigenous Person.

<u>The Definition of Sovereign:</u> {ME sovereign < L super, above, OVER} 1 above or superior to all others; chief; greatest; supreme 2 supreme in power, rank or authority 3 of or holding the position of ruler; royal; reigning 4 independents of all others {A Sovereign State or Country} 5 very effectual, as a cure or remedy.

<u>The Definition of Negros</u>: Negro, Black, Black person L Niger, Black} a member of "ANY" of the <u>"Indigenous"</u> dark-skinned peoples of Africa, living

chiefly south of the Sahara or a Person is having some Africa Ancestors; a black- Adj. Designating or of negroes.

The Definition of Negus: Amharic Negus King] [Historical] the title of the Wise Ruler of Ethiopia Negros- Island of the Central Philippines, between Cebu & Panay.

The Definition of Foreigner(s): a person or group from another Country, thought of as an outsider or Stranger, Alien.

The Definition of Colonizer: to find or establish a colony or colonies in 2 to settle (persons) in a colony *3 to place (voters) Illegally in (a district) to influence an election.

The Definition of Neanderthal: A widespread form of early European humans (Homo sapiens neanderthalensis) a Crude or Primitive reactionary; regressive, Uncivilized Person." See Mousterian; found at Le *Moustier,* Caves in Europe Germany designating or of a middle Paleolithic culture, associated with the Neanderthal cave people and characterized using Flaked hand Axes, Clubs, Scrapers, etc.

Historical Identity and Way of life of the Indigenous Negro American Population

The original name of America is "Gondwana and Amaraca, Amaru-Khans"
The proper term for the African Americans would be;
"Indigenous Negro of Gondwana" or Indigenous Negro of Amaraca

The Term: <u>Negro, Negus, Niger, Nigga, Naga's, Nagus, NTR, Nature</u>; derived from Ancient Kemet Egypt, Ethiopia, Mexico, Cambodia. Meaning: The Land of the Perfected Black ones, the Black Sun Gods, **Negro**- to Grow, to Learn, to Rise from the ground up, knee- grow, to rise, to <u>Gain Higher Consciousness</u>, i.e., Egyptian Sphinx human head rising out of the beast of ignorance and into Higher Consciousness -Negro. **Nagas**- the Divine Cosmic Force of the Black Serpent God of Asia, the Buddha- to Rise into Higher Consciousness, Nagas=**Sambo**- A Black God of the Cosmic Divine Forces. **Negus**- A Black King of Ethiopia or used as a Title of Sovereign Black people of <u>Great Knowledge-Wisdom- Negus</u>" (American English Dictionary Volume (4)

These Sacred Great Names are POWERFUL and as old as Time itself and, can only be used by the Melinated Ones.

<u>Skin Color:</u> Jet Black, Brown, Bronze, Copper, Reddish – Brown and Tan.

<u>Descendants Nationality</u>: Olmec's of America, Califia Blacks-California Blacks, Black Foot Cherokee, Creek Nation, Washita, and hundreds of

other Tribal Families throughout America, South America, Haiti, Bloodline Relatives to the Ancient Egyptians Pharaohs, Ethiopians, and throughout Mesopotamia.

Geographic Area: North/South America, Mexico, all surrounding Islands.

Bloodline Genetic type: Universal O- Negative, O- Positive, aka Alien Bloodline.

Date of Birth, Earth Civilization: Over 4- Million Years Ago on Earth.

Date of Birth of Human Existence: Over 3- Billion Years Ago throughout Planet Earth and Beyond the Galaxies of Space and Time.

World Civilization: The Negro American Tribes of the Ancient Olmecs, Queen Califia of California, Cherokee, Washita, and hundreds of other Melanated Tribes throughout America, Hawaii, Mexico, South America, Cuba, Puerto Rico, Hatti, Jamaica, and The Caribbean Islands. And, their relatives of Africa-ALKEBU-LAN- North/South Africa of Rome, Italy, Malta, Cypress, Greece, Spain, Portugal, and France. In which Europe is in fact, North Africa.

For more information on the Indigenous names and history. Google The Master Teachers and Honorable Historians: Dr. Eugene Adams, Bobby Hemmitt, C. Freeman EL. Dr. Phil Valentine, Dr, Delbert Blair, Dr, Z York, Young Pharaoh, Sara Suten Seti, Dane Calloway, and Kurimeo Ahau.

The Indigenous Negro, Behaviors, and Way of Life.

Most INA- Indigenous Negro Americans and A.A.-African American Population are Inherently equipped with Great Compassion, Humbleness, Great Respect, caring for other People of any Race. They usually go by the Natural order of Spirituality. Throughout our existence there was NO such thing as; Slavery, Prisons, Pedophilia, Homosexuality, Religion, Wars, Wars for Possessions & Land, nor the demand to pay for a Home, Food or Water. Every family and individual either had an abundance of wealth or had their proper basic needs met for sustainability. There were all kinds of Mystical Creatures and Exotic Animals that we highly respected. One Creature was made of a Lion body with huge Eagle wings on it back and a Falcon's head called "Griffins" They only lived in California and Lemuria.

Most of the Lands were Magically Enchanted where the Weather and Atmosphere Adored "You." Most Tribal Cultures traveled by Sea ships and by Spaceships to each other's Countries Cultivating Plant life and Animal Life.

They also Trade various Goods & Services, Gold, Silver, Precious Minerals, Various Materials, Tools & Supplies, Foods, Herbs & Spices, etc. They worked as Sea Voyagers, Manufactures, Blacksmiths, Construction builders of Homes, Temple Pyramids, Engineers, Doctors, Electrine, Scientists, etc. The Oceans Current is like a freeway traveling them quickly and directly to America, Mexico, South America and along the Caribbean shores. Indigenous Negro Americans are the Cultivators of America/Mexico and the surrounding Islands. Each Country had thriving Civilizations that goes back Millions of Years ago. Homes, Temples, Universities, Shops and Energy Pyramids were constructed in various States throughout America. Their Marriages and Procreation were common intermingling with the Ancient Black Egyptians, North Black Africans of Rome, Greece, Spain, Portugal, Cypress, Ethiopians, Ivory Coast, Ghanaians, Israel, Jordan, and Judea. Therefore, some not all but some of our DNA is a mixture of either South American, North/South African, Caribbean Islanders, Haitians, Jamaicans, and Black Asians.

There was No Other Race of People who existed at that time" Not until some 12- thousand years ago. And those were the Pale Asians and Aztecs Mayans, Indian Americans who Originated out of Alaska- Siberia, Russia, and Mongolia. The Aztecs claimed that the Ancient Pyramids in America/ Mexico and Other Ancient artifacts, advanced Tools, Craved Stone Heads of the Ancient Olmecs were already there when they first arrived in Mexico and South America. Written Testimony from numerous Explores, the Spaniard Explores and Christopher Columbus, and his Minions. States that there were Hispanic men who walked with two other Negros Americans who had Gold Tipped Spares that lead them to Millions of Negro Tribes throughout the Americas".

According to Professor Historian Ivan Van Sertima, and Dr. John Henrik Clarke, Ashra Kwesi, Historian researcher Dane Calloway, Kurimeo Ahau and many other Prominent Historians all states; From the African Pharaohs of Egypt as Gold Exporters/Importers to the Ivory Coast and Ghana, to the Sky Gods Olmec's of America and Mexico, to the Serpent Nagas of Asia-Cambodia and Thailand. They all had their own set of Rules, Laws Policies and Respect for one another that Carved in Stone. Sacred to Sustain itself for the Future of its "Off-Spring Descendants. According to the United States Congress Archives Library, the name they used to call Black Americans were "Indians"

For more information about the 10 million Indigenous Negro's of America. There's a 1757 to 1910 Book named, The Origin and the Meaning of the Name California" Calafia the Black Queen of the Island of California. written by; Officers, President, Professor George Davidson, PH. D., Sc., D., LL, D University of California) Vice President: Hon. Ralph C. Harrison, Directors John Partridge, Henry Lund, and Harry Durbrow. Or simply go to the United States Congress Archives and look up Indian Cherokee Tribes National Law Book 1770-1837

<u>Is Europeans Indigenous to Europe? Is Europe, really Europe? I think not.</u>

Look at a world map. There appears to be a small lake that connects between Africa and the alleged name of Europe. But is it Europe? Not geographically speaking it is Not Europe at all. It's North Africa. North Africa of Greece, Rome, Italy. Malta, Cyprus, Spain, France, and Portugal.

When you consider the fact that North Africa was and still is lived by 50% of Black and Brown Indigenous people.

Then one can assume that the alleged named "Europe" was made up by the "White Europeans" in the 1300-1600s. The people of Africa who lived there had a different name for their region; Europe is not the correct name of Europe because it connects to Africa. Not even Africa is the correct name. According to the Honorable Dr. Ben Yosef Jochannan the correct name of Africa is ALKEBU-LAN- and the actual name of America is Gondwana and Amaraca, Amaru-Khans" everything that we know today always has an original title to it.

According to the U.S. Congress Archives, the so-called Native Indians, Mexicans, and Chinese all originated from Siberia Alaska, Russia. The Mexicans and Indians coming from Siberia Alaska migrated into Canada and then America, and South America. Whom all discovered an advanced civilization of Melinated Black, Brown and Reddish-Brown Indigenous People known as African Americans. The proper term for the African Americans would be Indigenous Negro of Gondwana" or Indigenous Negro Amaraca" existing in their own Country, Continents from around the world for over 3-Million years before the existence of any other race being on the Planet. The National Geographic of Studies said that the first Black person was found in Africa and in Europe over 1 Billion years ago. And the Ancient Olmecs Heads that were found throughout Mexico are said to Millions of years old as well. In fact, the Aztec claim that the Mayan Pyramids were there before they Arrived in Mexico and South America.

Most people believe from misinformation propaganda and Television that Mayans Pyramids were used only for Sacrificing people by cutting their heads off. But that's not what it was originally used for. They were used for UFO landing Pads. That's right, the Ancient Olmecs were Land Cultivators, they were "The Planters" and would bring back all kinds of Exotic Plantlife, Wildlife and even people from other Planets such as Mars before the Planet was destroyed on the surface. Also, from other Planets as well and Cultivate this land to what it is today. They would park their Spaceship throughout America in places like Cairo Illinois, the Arizona Grand Canyon, Memphis, Malibu you name it. Wherever there's a city there's a Pyramid covered up. Some Pyramids can't be covered up no matter what you do. It was meant to show all its Glory.

You probably even think that Mountains are just plain ole rock stone hills huh?

Nope, believe it not the Mountains are "Petrified Human Giants" and some of the largest Mountains that you see all over America and the world are in fact, giant cut off tree stumps. That's right "We are the Little People" well we became the little people. But the giants use to live on the earth.

So, in other words, the Fairy Tale "Jack and the Bean Stalk" wasn't so farfetched. You see this is what happens when the worst types of people take over a country. They strip away everything of your historical knowledge and identity. That's vitally important to your way of life and understanding of things. You don't have to, believe me, you can find out for yourself.

You can start by looking at certain information portals on YouTube. Type in "Are Mountains really Tree Stumps? Or "What is Petrified Human Mountains". But you must be careful when looking at information on YouTube. YouTube is like shopping for clothes at a Thrift Store. Every now and then you'll always find some Great Stuff.

Anyway, where was I...Oh yea "Historical identity of White People"

This Document is Ordained by True Accurate Evidence of Historical & Current accounts that is written herein. All keywords and information mentioned can be easily found at your local Library, U.S. Congress Archives, Public Museum, The English Webster Dictionary. National Geographic's. Books and Magazines.

Christopher Columbus and the UFO

On October 11th, 1492 Christopher Columbus his minions and a Spanish explore name Guettara's wrote a Journal that tells how they were lost at sea and a Round Bright Disk shaped came out of the sea. It hovered over the water for a while and then led their ship to America. Right around the time the Gun Powder and Guns were invented. They, of course, slaughtered the Indigenous population throughout. The Alien/UFO did not interfere, they stood back and watched. And so, the question is; why would they allow this to happen to innocent people? Did the UFO that leads them to the Americas not know what Christopher's intention was?

Of course, they knew. They know exactly what Christopher intention was in coming to America. Alien Beings are responsible for the creation of his entire bloodline race. But why would they unleash such a savage race of people upon the innocent Indigenous population? Since they are watching over all of us, what would be the purpose of watching the destruction of a certain race? One of the answers to that fundamental question could be answered through the following;

It is mentioned in the book "Encounters" page 274 titled "They Call Themselves the Planters" In that book, it speaks of a woman who was abducted by a Large Spaceship in the Bay Area of California. Inside the Spaceship were two very tall Black men who were in charge, she asked the men why were there so many beautiful black people on this Ship? and why were some groups of black people hysterical and other groups were overjoyed with happiness? The two tall "Black Beings" told her the Black people had "Different Souls" and that they placed their "Children" (Black people in America) in the roughest of circumstances for a "High Service". They (the Beings) came before around 40,000 years ago and they picked up many of their "Children". This time it's the biggest return ever. And we're picking our "Children" up from various "Impoverished Ghetto areas" for a "High Purpose" under severe Oppressed circumstances". They continued, "some of our "Children" (the Black people) on the ship were hysterical because there are Nuclear Bombs being dropped everywhere, and we were picking them up right when the bombs were landing". The Abductee was taken on board in the '70s. The event that the "Black Beings" were referring to is 2019 through 2024.

Throughout Ancient history in just about every Black cultural from around the world seems to point the importance of gaining "Higher Consciousness" this is the only way that a Soul can grow at a much faster rate. Eventually, the Soul would place itself on a higher level of existence throughout Dimensions. That's why the Ancient Egyptians put so much emphasis on Life After Death. Because the only thing that's important to them is to Nurture the Soul. And in order to do that, the soul must live in rash environments i.e. oppression, slavery, tyranny, corruption, injustices)

Which leads us all to this "Orchestrated Human Masquerade" that we call Life. So, the overall picture here is that somebody must play the Evil Villain. While others must play the victims and the watchers of the victims. For the purpose of obtaining "Higher Consciousness" that allows the soul to grow. And we learn through all kinds of good and bad human experiences. I mean after all, "What's the use of a god who only dwells in Heaven? A god-like person or a god in training must refine him or herself "Under Extreme Pressure" for the Soul to reach a much higher level throughout the many Dimensions that travel and live on. For more information about other historical UFO involvement, Google; the Ancient Alien History Channel, the Book of the Encounters written by Edith Fiore, Ph. D a professional Psychologist and Author. The book "The Threat" written by David M. Jacobs, Ph.D. Professional Psychologist and Author.

Historical Identity and Way of life Khazarians- Viking Fugitive Slaves- aka Europeans.

Skin Color: Dark Pink, Light Pink, White, Pale White.

Nationality: Caucasians, White Asiatic Khazarians Descendants, Asiatic aka; White Vikings, White Romans, White Race.

Geographic Area: Northeast Asia, Originated from KAZAKHSTAN, Mongolia of the Caucasus Mountain of Russia Helsinki, Bulgaria, Hungary, Belarus, Ukraine, Slovakia, Lithuania.

Bloodline Genetic DNA Origin: Canine, Reece's Monkey mixed with another Human, Origin of Half Human, Half Beast, i.e. NEANTHERALS Then the Grey Alien interbreed with the Neanderthals

Date of Birth of Human Existence: 4 -Thousand Years Ago.

Bloodline Cultures: The North East Asiatic, The Ancient White Hyksos, Hittites, White Libyans, White Assyrians, The white Romans, The English, The White Spaniards, The Portuguese, The White Jew-ish people, The Russians, The Germans, The Christians, Khazarian Vikings Migration into "North Africa of Europe" then eventually into South America, America: 1200 C.E through1900.

Business Corp. D.O. B: August 1790, April 1933 formed in Philadelphia on Stolen Land. Known as Foreign: United States Federal Government Corporation Congress Assembled and all its Unwarranted Executive Branches.

In Biblical Terms: Ashkenazi Jew = Jew-ish Meaning, they are Not the Original Jews of Judea but are in fact, "The Synagogue of Satan" Colonized Northern Africa of Europe coming out from the Village of Helsinki Caucasus Mountains.

These white European Races are actually "Viking Fugitive Slaves of Helsinki" all originated from North Asia Mongolia, from Kazakhstan, Russia to Poland. A primitive Savage Warlike people who'd made their living <u>enslaving their own race of people</u>, Murdering, Raping, Stealing and Pillaging their Towns and Villages in the 4th Century 500 A.D. From Northern Caucasus Mountains, Ukraine, Romania, Poland, etc. To hide their Satan Horns, they eventually converted into Judaism Religion= "Viking- Jew-ish People." In 1 B.C.E they immigrated then colonized Northern Africa of Rome, Greece, Italy, Malta, Cyprus, Spain, France, and Portugal. Yes, North Africa is Rome, Italy, Spain, etc.

The Mental Comprehension, Behaviors and Way of Life

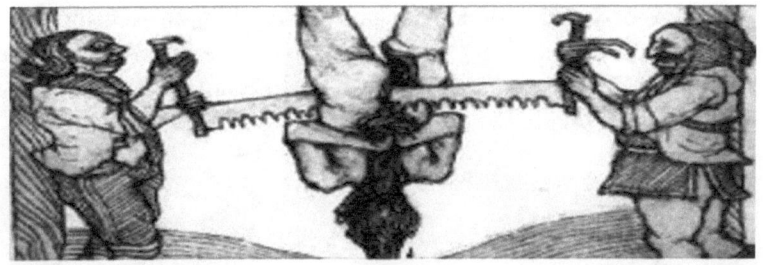

It's a proven fact that Enslavement came from the Europeans their race of people is a normal way of life for them. These Viking's thirst for War, Blood, and Possessions has gotten so bad that most were sent to Prison as Slaves themselves. Around 1100 A. D. Then eventually were kicked out and escaped from their town and villages. And migrated into Poland, Norway, Sweden, Finland, United Kingdom. Thousands of these Fugitive Viking Slaves escaped and immigrated into Northern Africa of Rome, Greece, Italy, France Spain, Portugal. Spreading more mayhem and destruction through various States.

They have caused what is known as "The 100 War between England and France". Most of those Prisoner Viking Slaves of Khazarians Race of Helsinki) Eventually escaping as a Fugitive Runaway Slaves. They set the seal to pillage other Countries across the Seas finding their way to South America, Mexico, and America. In which Christopher Columbus bloodline of (Viking Fugitive Slaves of Helsinki) and his minions, the Spaniards and other Viking Fugitive Slave Explore discovered that there are Millions of Negro Americans living throughout what would become the 13 Colonies.

They eventually saw Millions of Negros living throughout California, Mexico, Kansas, Michigan, Florida, Louisiana, etc. Since 1600's-1900's begun the total takeover of attacks, genocide, and destruction on ALL Indigenous Negro Americans as well as the newly arrived Siberia Alaska Indians and Hispanic's of Russia, Canada. Have all suffered by the hands of the Runaway Fugitive Viking Slaves. Today they wear suits and tie.

It's even in the Bible Rev 2:9 I know thy works, tribulation, and poverty. But thou are Rich. And I know the Blasphemy of them which say they are Jews and are NOT but are the "Synagogue of Satan" And then when you look at how incredibly Dysfunctional and Danger our Society it is today. It does not take a Rocket Scientist to figure out the Obvious. Now I'm not saying that all White People are Bad. In fact, the sitting President Donald J. Trump is doing a Pretty Good Job in getting rid of the "Evil Top CIA and FBI Agents and even some of the top Democrats and Republicans running scared. Those unwarranted government entities for many, many years created hell on earth for the Indigenous Negro Americans. Whether anyone wants to admit it or not. It's the absolute Truth.

Why was the Constitution, Congress and the Declaration formed?

QUARTERING ACT 1765

- Following the French & Indian War, British troops remained in the colonies to defend against foreign threats.
  - The Quartering Act required colonies to provide food and housing for British troops
  - Colonial assemblies voted to refuse to supply British soldiers

They labeled themselves as various nationalities such as; the United Kingdom, Norway, Sweden, Portugal, France, Europe of North Africa. These People were enslaved they owed debts to each other. Such as the white Settlers (U.S. Congress Assembled) owed a debt, Servitude to the British for wars that took place in the UK before arriving in America.

The British believe that the Settlers (U.S. Congress Assembled) had to return to the United Kingdom to finish their debt and their "Servitude. And if they didn't return to the British Council Government, they would consider that as "Treason". So, the "Settlers" in America are in fact "Fugitives Slaves and Bloodline of the Ancient white Viking" The British even forced their way into the Fugitive Viking Settlers home for refuge and hospitality. This caused great conflict between the two based on both parties acquiring individual Freedoms, Respect and boundaries. On stolen land, none could live in harmony with one another. Being "Civilized" towards one another did not exist hostility and anger grew.

That led to a massacre which led to the Civil War of the 13 States being taken over and colonized by the foreigners aka Viking Fugitive Slaves of Helsinki. After the War of 1776 ended the Viking Fugitive Slave Settlers formed what is now known as the Constitution and the Declaration. Both were formed to stop the British from taking them back to Prison as deserters of their regiment. It was also written to "Teach" all foreign white Settlers on How to be "Civilized," They wrote it specifically for the 13 colonies and NOT for all other States. With the written words of "Every Man is Created Equal" Every man has the right to Life, Liberty, and the Pursuit of Happiness." Who were they referring this too? During that time the Land was being stolen from the Indigenous Negros as they were criminally being enslaved. They certainly weren't talking to the Indigenous Negro Americans. So, who was the Constitution and Declaration originally written for?

It was written for those who were voided of all Wisdom, Logical Reasoning, and Respect for boundaries. These groups knew that their own people are voided of this fundamental reasoning and reality. They automatically had to be given some life information of how to "Civilized. In the same manner, as to how the Bible was created by the Vikings. Religion is only created by the Uncivilized person who wishes to be Civilized. I mean after all, what would a person need a Bible for if they already live in Heaven? And it's obvious that we are not in heaven.

That Indigenous would not need a Bible because compassion, understanding, common sense and Respect is embedded within his or her DNA. 90% of the Indigenous Negro has this DNA. Which is understandable to why they were placed on the earth first before any religions and before any other race.

The Bible and the Constitution were originally written by the Uncivilized, for the Uncivilized people. So, if you happen to visit another Planet and stumble across a Bible, or any kind of human civilized instructions? Any race of people who must be taught how to be Civilized should never have the right to rule over another Country. Laws, Civilized instructions can only be written by one who is Indigenous to that Land. As we can see today much Political conflict in America. Still being fought on stolen land in the presence of the neglected and ignored Indigenous Negro Americans. Even though their own Constitutional Laws were intended to give their people Equal Rights, Life, Liberty for the Pursuit of Happiness has all been proven to be a mere Fantasy for the white race.

How did these Viking Fugitive Slave- Colonizer Become so Wealthy?

Those hard-working, pull-themselves-up-by-their-bootstraps Viking Fugitive Slaves" experienced at least 10 windfalls in their history:

1) Land: The Civil War was all about Land Stealing, never about freeing the Kidnapped Enslaved Negro Americans. And they fault each other to death over Land that wasn't theirs, to begin with! The largest farmlands across America were stolen. From Virginia, Texas, Oklahoma, Louisiana to California. Moreland was stolen than in all of Europe and China! White Colonizers took it from the Indigenous Negro Americans and forced the Victims to build their Oppressors homes, businesses, they made Cotton King of the industry along with, Sugar, Tobacco Plants and Railroads, Steel mills and much, much more. Of all the products and services that we all see today.

2) Labor: at cut rates from enslaved Indigenous Negro Americans: Manufacturers workers, Construction workers House Maids, Yard Landscapers, Farm Workers, Raising Cattle all done by FREE LABOR, etc. Indigenous Negros are *still* markedly underpaid even when you take education into account.

3) Money: much of the wealth of the Viking Fugitive Slave British Empire. The British Empire went broke fighting Hitler. This is where most of their

money went. It went to America, nearly all of it to Viking Fugitive Slave White Settlers, NOT to the Indigenous Negro fighters and Pilots who help win the war in defeating Hitler's armies. Without the Redtails, Viking Fugitive Slave white settlers living in America would've lost the War.

Today the Viking Fugitive Slave -Colonizers who think it was all just a matter of hard work and the right values are far removed from all reality. Today much of the Viking Fugitive Slave- Settlers narrow mindset of history. Commonly states ("None of my family owned slaves", "My grandfather came to America with only $25 in his pocket") If hard work and the right values were enough, then why on earth did their forefathers leave their own Countries of Kazakhstan Helsinki? Just to live the rest of their lives in a foreign land across the ocean. Because they knew that hard work, the right values and morals were simply not within the scope of their understanding. 85% of the white race who are in office are completely avoided by all Common Sense, Logical reasoning, and Compassion. To the point that they illegally formed the U.S. to be a Corporation.

And any person with a brain knows that you cannot Incorporate Land. You Cannot Incorporate Laws, You Cannot Incorporate Government. They call themselves Americans when in fact they are all "U.S. Citizens.

The Atlantic Slave Trade Story is the Biggest American Lie Ever Written in Human History!

The Atlantic Kidnaped Slave Trade Act is a Horrible Fictional Story. That was written and published in every School Book, Press article, Postcards, Magazines even in religion. For the purpose of taking away the Land, Farming, Business Valuable Possessions, and Mineral Resources. Away from the Indigenous Negro American Population. Throughout the Centuries these Viking Fugitive Slave-Settlers used brainwashing techniques such as Religion, Post Cards, Newsletters, Churches and now Television, News Media and Movies shown throughout the world. Convincing every one of the Biggest Lie Ever Written in Human Story.

Remember, these groups of Fugitive Vikings Slaves lived and studied in Northern Africa of Rome, Greece, Portugal, Spain, etc. They tried to understand the teachings of Ancient Kemet Egypt and stole parts of the Egyptians life story placing it in the Bible then distorting the Truth. They even found our Sacred names; Negus, Negro, Nagas, Nagus being used throughout Africa, Cambodia, Ethiopia, and Rome. They heard the word "Nagus in Rome, Negus in Ethiopia, Negro in Mexico, Nagas or Nigga in Thailand. Being said by our own Ancestors since the beginning of time. It's one of the most Powerful names in the Ancient Human language. And, yet the Fugitive Viking Slaves have come to America and used it in an extremely disrespectful manner. Which to this very day if the Negro of any age hears our Sacred name being said disrespectfully? Then we are instantly enraged and compelled to choke, punch, and twist the life out of the person that said it. Not caring about any consequences because the notion of hurting that person is worth more than Gold.

Throughout History books, newsletters, postcards, Television Claiming that the English, Portuguese, Polk's, Sweden's, Portuguese and French all took part in the Atlantic Kidnaped Enslavement Act. They've promoted throughout the Centuries that they took over 10 Million of the most Powerful Africans from various parts of West Africa such as; Ghana, Sierra Leone, Cameroon, Liberia, Nigeria. All claiming that they sailed on Cargo Ships that can only fit 20 people. In wooden ships going back and forth through the Treacherous Seas to the Americas. Without the resistance of millions of other Horrified African fightings back?

(Think about it) The history books that they wrote are saying that a small group of White men- Viking Fugitive Slaves came into Africa and stole 10 million of the most Powerful Africans in the World. From an African regional area that the White Foreigners have NEVER been too before. And, yet they claim that they sailed Back and Forth stealing millions of men, women, and children. Without the help of other million relatives that would've normally been waiting for them with Machetes Blades at the Gate. You can't even fit that many people in that type of ship, and do you know how many ships you need for 10 million people? And, yet they have not perverse one Slave ship to show proof that the slave Trade happened. They could not sail back and forth to steal that many people without being met up with powerful opposition. And if another Africa Tribe or a Black Arab tribe was helping the Vikings Fugitives? Those Tribes would've been Killed first, and their villages would've been destroyed.

And guess what? You cannot travel the seas today wearing only underwear as the Africans "Allegedly" did. They would've been frozen to death! They only show "Fictional Drawings" of half-naked Africans on ships. But, in reality, it's too cold to travel for a long period of time. About time they reach the shores of America they would've had human popsicles on board. Even Fugitive Slave Christopher Columbus wrote in his Journal that him and his Minions damn near died from Hypothermia and Typhus [Typhus- infectious disease caused by Bug Lice, Fleas crawling underneath the skin, also known as Morgellons and Lyme Disease] Christopher Columbus and 60% of the white race suffer from Bug Disease that is produced from their Blood Cells till this very day 50% of white people suffer from the Bug Disease. [Look it up and see for yourself, Google Morgellons and Lyme Disease]

So, there is no way they could sail back and forth for decades having those type of diseases. Remember the "English Fugitive Slave" greeted the so-called "Natives Americans" with their diseased Bug Infested Blankets.

Because they knew what their Sickness could be used as a weapon against innocent people of taking over their land.

According to Common Sense and all Logical reasoning "The Alleged" Atlantic Kidnaped Slave Trade" would've been impossible to achieve. And without any evidence to prove that there were Slave ships that could hold thousands makes the Slave Trade story a Fictional one. Go ahead try and find a 1619-1865 Slave ship that could hold less than 25 thousand people. Try and find one that could hold two thousand people. Only cargo ships were active during that time and that was only used for transporting Goods, not people. Some people say, "Well the Slave Trade was Big Business," and that's the traditional way of doing things back then." No, it was not, first off, Slavery never existed in Africa or America's before to the Arabs and Viking Fugitive Slave Colonization. Slavery was no more popular then what it is today. It was not allowed since there was no such thing as Slavery in Africa America, South America, Cuba, Haiti and so on.

The Honorable Ashra Kwesi Master Teacher of Ancient Kemet takes people on tours to Egypt three times a year. To show the truth of what's written on the Pyramid walls. And it clearly shows a battled ensued between the Pharaohs, the Vikings, and the Black Arabs. In which the Pharaohs was telling them all to get off their land and to leave his people alone! Not "Let my People Go" as so commonly used in the Bible. But, all of us must determine what is Fantasy Fiction and what is Fact. It was the Viking Fugitive Slaves that migrated into Rome of Africa on Ships and Colonized Rome, Spain, Portugal, etc. Then later arrived on Ships Colonizing America. Therefore, it was NOT the Indigenous Negro population who came on Ships to America. No! It was the Viking Fugitive Slaves who are the "African Americans" that came on ships and immigrated themselves into America coming from Rome of Africa—slaughtering the Elders and most of the Parents. Then they brainwashed the "Young" reversing the truth and telling the greatest propaganda lies in Human History!

A well-known Historian Researcher named Dane Calloway have pointed this out on his YouTube channel called; "I'm just here to make you think.com"

In 2016 he Stated;

"On all Virginia State Metal Plaques WT-1 States "The first Africans in English America arrived at James Town in August 1619 A- <u>Dutch man-of War</u> captured them from the Spanish who had enslaved them and sold them to the Virginia Colonists. The <u>"Twenty"</u> and odd "Africans some of whom had been given Spanish named may have been treated like indentured servants and later freed after their periods of servitude expired." It Does Not Say on "ANY" of the 2013 updated Virginia Plaques WT-1) that there was a total of 10 -Million Africans stolen from Africa and brought to America. It just states that "Twenty" was stolen." ---Dane Calloway"

Here is another one of Dane Calloway video explained on YouTube. I do NOT own the copyrights of these words. These are Dane Calloway word for word. The Story of a man named: **"Who is Melville J. Herskovits?**

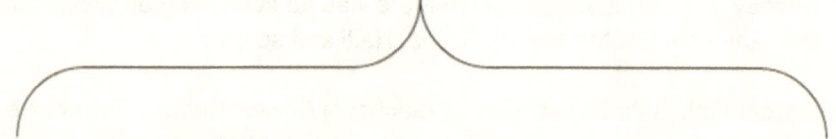

Dane Calloway speaks- "Melville Herskovits was born on September 10, 1895, in Bellefontaine Ohio to two Jew-ish immigrants' parents who immigrated from parts of Europe to Northern America during the mid-1800s. His mother Henrietta Hart was an immigrant from Germany, and his father Herman Herskovits was an immigrant from Hungary. Melville attended the Jewish College institution and later transferred to the University of Chicago at a time where anthropology was heavily influenced by the deceitful hidden agenda of industrialism alone with Political European Colonialism where Soto scientist theory was not only praised by one group of people but, justified for its subjections of all non-white people.

It is called the "Illusion" of Power" whereas this illusion is a group of people who somehow believe that they are superior over others. What is also important to note here is that there are multiple different entities that are man-made "History of Illusion" Along with various types of "Science, Technology, and Religions." These are all "Social Engineering Experiments" were cultivated by the same one group of people to compel the masses to adopt their ideology along with their manipulative rhetorical motivates. Before world war, I began in a speech directed to some credited businessmen.

President Woodrow Willison stated that hence fourth public policy would be geared to provide public education tailor to producing industrial worker who did not question orders and was skilled in only basic manual labor and that a liberal education would be reserved only for a small elite.

> "I do not inveigh against higher education; I simply maintain that the sort of education the "Colored People" of the south stand most in need of, is elementary and industrial.
>
> They should be instructed for the work to be done."
> "Timothy Thomas Fortune"

This programs the individuals to become prone with their limits to literal and critical thinking capabilities. Not only were these same malicious and deceitful tactics were used in the past, but these detrimental effects currently being affected as normal in today's society!

> "The purpose of Compulsory Education is to deprive the common people of their Commonsense." Gilbert K. Chesterton"

This form of role reversal began with Charles Darwin and his followers. When they began to promote and teach the theory of "Evolution" during the 1800s. As you may know "A theory of "Evolution" is a scientific Mythoi in which Charles Darwin "Thinks" the process of natural selection and Soto science which Blatant Racist is absolutely disinformation that he cultivated about the world's population.

Now the real question is, why would he do this? Well, it's NOT about whether a man came from monkeys as society would want you to believe. So, people can argue about this fictitious theory whenever it brought up. No, it's more about the different traits of the human populations, how different traits conferred different rates of survival and reproduction and how these traits can be passed down from generation to generation.

Now you might be asking, so what does this have to do with our "History Being Told in Reverse?" And the answer to that is "EVERYTHING" because Charles Darwin created this theory of evolution not because of Apes" but because he is a part of it genetically."

In other words, Charles Darwin Soto Science Theory was used to manipulate people into believing that they evolved from Apes, but in all actuality. He was endeavoring to figure out "Where his Species of people came from.

This module would go onto formulating how these group of collective off-Spring will be able to continue forward in successive generations as the quote "The Survival of the Fittest" See you must understand were Europe is located before it was called Europe. That particular land mass was and still is a part of Africa. And all this correlates with some of the many things that were told to you in "Reverse"

Like for example; The out of Africa Theory" now keep in mind I just explain to you the hidden details behinds Charles Darwin theory and just like his theory of evolution the entire out of Africa theory" Is merely nothing but an indoctrinated form of manipulative Soto storytelling that was cultivated by the like of a self-proclaim fictitious bigoted scientist named "Melville Jean Herskovits" a so-called Anthropologist of the early 1900s.

Melville is solely responsible for expanding the lie of storytelling on which in turn it was later considered to be American History by completely reversing to records of Historic information and creating a fictional story about African Slaves immigrating to Americas by way of the Spaniards in the 1500s. This story is known as "The Middle Passage" However, before Melville fiction story, no information existed in history that mentioned not the so-called "Negros" of the American Lands came from Africa.

For example, according to an English immigrant by the name of "Noah Webster" who was the Author of the Webster's English Language Dictionary the year 1828 definition of American is quote "A Native of America, originally applied to the Aboriginals, or Copper Colored Races found here in America by the Europeans, but now applied to the descendants of Europeans born in America.

"Also, Melville "Allegedly" took a trip somewhere in Africa, meaning, that there are no records of this) such a story that he gathered up stating that he took a few artifacts, observed a few tribes and a few cultures and dubbed it as Africanism. Then traveled back to the Americas wrote a book called "The Myth of the Negro Past" and published it in 1942 in the "Fictional Sectional" where he claimed that the people of color in America somehow lost connection with their cultural past during the "Middle Passage" from Africa to the Americas. More importantly,

Melville taught many so-called "Black Leaders" this same "Out of Africa Theory" Manipulative of indoctrination promoted the idea that Negros residing in America are all somehow the descendants of Africans. Sole on the fact that we all share the same hue of complexion and that's it"

"Is it safe to say that the Irish from Ireland who has the same hue complexion as the Asiatic is the same direct bloodline descendants as the white Asiatic's from Mongolia? Probably not. Because there are many different races within humans."

The Harvard taught sociologist and one the co-founders of the NAACP and the first so-called person of color to even earn a doctrine at this time named "W.E.B Du Bois took this fictitious idea to new heights as though he was considered to be a person of color providing another side of social engineering influenced amongst people that shared his same hue of complexion. In, fact Frans Bass influenced W.E.B Du Bois and his teaching even while being a professor of sociology at the Economics in history at Atlanta University Frans Boss taught Melville and other students this same Manipulative false teaching to all Colleges.

By the earlier 1900s American industrialist recognized that republican education was the most useful means to socially engineer the American population to suit the purpose of industrial capitalism. From these evil ideal local networks of corporation's foundations university education and psychological departments educational crediting broads and governmental agencies of every kind arose to oversee the implementation of the blueprint of this ambitious but yet so <u>Devastatingly Evil</u> Social engineering project these entities included organizations such as the Rockefeller Foundation, the Carnegie Foundation, the Columbia Teachers college. The University of Chicago, the National trading Labs Institute NTL, the National Education Association NEA, and the U.S. Office of education 1947 now known as The Department of Education, Andrew Carnegie, JP Morgan, John D. Rockefeller and Henry Ford were the key contributors in intraductal architects of this American educational system of forced schooling. According to Lee D. Baker an author, Cultural anthropologist drew suspicious correlations between anatomical features and suppose behavior traits of the various races.

The people like Melville and the U.S. Government along with the U.S. Public School System and Library of Congress. Would like everyone to believe that the Lands of America were un-occupied before their arrivals *into America. But the truth is they were occupied by our Great Grand Parents and Ancestors and NOT these people they were referring to Native Americans. The pale skinned Native Indians are not native to America at all. They originated out of Alaska Siberia and Russia.*

Immigrating into Canada and later into the Americas. Our Ancestors were NOT pale skinned people. But, Black to Brown Copper, Bronze colored complexions People. The "Out of Africa" theory along with these fraudulent DNA Government test from the 1900s worked hand and hand for one big reason because they were created by the same group of people that forced everyone to believe that the Black to Copper Colored people of America came from Africa. When in fact, Millions of these Europeans did not arrive in America until the late 1700s, hence the reason why the U.S. Census did not begin to population count until the year 1790."

"Dane Calloway" @ I'm just here to make you think.com"

10 Million Africans Stolen from Africa is Impossible!

So, if 10-Million Africans were "Allegedly" stolen? Then how come they never stated "Where they Supposedly" took these Africans from? Like what City areas did they steal 10- Million Africans from? If, you can steal 10- Million Africans? You're going to know the exact Tribal names and the exact neighborhood. Because you can't just go into a large village and just start snatching up people that you have never seen or met before. And, if you did snatch up a bunch of people you could not come back fourth picking up over nine million more.

How is it that we find the Ancient bodies of the Egyptian Pharaohs, Ramses, Tutankhamun, The Great Goddess Hatshepsut, Nefertiti, Khufu, and his Noah's Ark Ship. Including all their Artifacts, Furniture, Hair furnishings, Shoes, Clothing, Chess Game Boards and their Coffins that dates back over 50 thousand years. In which all materials are currently displayed at the Egyptian, British and American Museums today. And, yet not one Kidnapped Slave Ship in America could be found. That would date back only 100 Years ago. Studies have shown that the only Cargo ships that were built in the Americas were made from American Wood by the Indigenous American forced Labor. They were forced to load up American goods of food, Cotton, imports and export of Stolen Ancient Artifacts, Precious Minerals, Stones, Gold, Silver, Foods, Plants, Clothing Shoes. And ship them to all parts of Europe, France, England, Poland, Germany.

This ultimately ended the sustainability, happiness, wellbeing for the Indigenous Negro Americans. Including all Caribbean Islanders, Hawaiians, Cubans, Haitians, Jamaicans, South Americans, Cambodians, etc. Remember just because something that was written in A.D. or B.C. era doesn't mean that they didn't know how to use fake propaganda to lie and cheat their way through life. For example; Did you know that the so-called "Jew-ish Holocaust was propagandizing 6 years before the German War Holocaust even happened?

That's right the Bloodline Fugitive Slaves of Helsinki, Kazakhstan and Uzbekistan were living in such impoverished conditions that anyone living over there during that time would easily label it as Cold Hell on Earth. They begged their government for money such much that they ended up making up a fabricated story about them being placed in concentration camps and being rounded up and shot. And what they want was the Country of Israel and now they want Palestine. They wanted to live a better life knowing that the Sun never shines on their Cold desolate Country of Kazakhstan and Uzbekistan. They wanted to live in a warm beautiful country where the food growth and precious metals are abundant. Look it up and see for yourself. Google it or type in keywords like: Was the Holocaust Fabricated? Some might say "Oh is that where you get your information from is the Public Library, Museums, National Geographic, Congress Archives, Google or YouTube, and the Smithsonian? Yes, the People who live there and is part of that culture who have first -hand experience of what is happening in their world. Are the same ones who are uploading the information on Google and YouTube. You don't have to travel to Egypt to see if Pyramids over there or not.

The Current Grievance Statement & Solution Proposal- To the Governor of the Federal Reserve Systems

The "Current Problem Statement and Grievance Proposal" was presented to the Federal Reserve and U.S. Congress Assembled. On June 7th, 2010 and again on September 6th, 2018 It was present to them for the purpose to review what is outlined and to fund the proposal to eliminating Homelessness and Poverty that is contributed to all sort of government crimes. This proposal details what the problems are and gives instructions on how to eliminate the problems. That they themselves have created through their own government Law Policies. The board of Governors of the Federal Reserve System is design to take the consumerisms and the spending profits from "The People" and give part of that money to their Military, Police Departments and Banking Systems. And herd it all to themselves. Not giving it back to the people that need it the most.

The Federal Reserve brings in well over $5 Trillion every 2 years. They often send out to the press that they lost $9 Trillion and they don't know where it went. After sending out my Funding Proposal plan, I only received an Email from the Federal Reserve acknowledging that they received my Proposal. Therefore, they have the Solution BILL to the current problems but refuse to do anything about it. And this is what you call "Government Corruption and Tyranny"

This Grievance Letter is Address To:
The Board of Governors of the Federal Reverse System.
Office of the Ombudsman Federal Reserve Board Systems
20th & Streets, NW, Mail Stop -28
Washington, D.C. 20551
Office Phone: (800) 337-0429 or (202) 452-3000

I'm Presenting all documents relating to the initial Grievance Statement Letter that was Emailed on September 6th, 2018. Regarding; Funding Request Approval. Documents Includes:

Herein, September 11, 2018, Grievance Letter, California State Senate Bill Act Request, Company Business Plan, K.M.R.E.C.D. Law Decree, Successful Service Social Programs Inc.

Required Funding request for the development of Katherine's Magical Revitalization, Inc Initiatives. And/or request Approval as a Bill Act Law" of Great Urgency for ALL Americans.

IntroductionGrievance Statement Letter

Filing a Formal Grievance against the California State Senate and the Board of Governors of the Federal Reserve System.

I, Katherine Irvin hereby state the following Complaint/Grievances:

Katherine Irvin, the Founder/CEO/Manager of Katherine's Magical Kingdom Inc, and the Successful Service Social Program Inc. formed in Los Angeles California since 2007. Both companies are designed to change America for the better. It's the development of Self- Governing Prosperous Economic Communities. Communities that are like what Dr. Martin Luther King referred to as;

"**The Promise Land**".

Katherine's Magical Revitalization Economic Development Service Inc. is designed for Long-term Economic Growth on a massive global level. Would reach Annual Sale Profits of over $3 Trillion through Nation-Worldwide Economic Consumerisms System. Half of the proceed would back into the communities that are most impoverished. This service is designed for the U.S. Government to admit into Law as a "Bill Act" by Congress. Because it is the Solution of eliminating 80% of Severe Mental, Physical Stress and Strain that's contributed by Poverty, Homelessness, Various Illegal Law Policy, Police Brutality, Mass Incarceration, and Government Corruption and Abuse against its citizens.

Numerous times I have sent my Company's Bill Act documents to former and Current United States Presidents, Senators, local State Legislators, and Local Congressmen since 2007-2018. My latest submission to the State Senate was submitted by Postal Certified Mail on January 4th, February 5, 2018, is denied or ignored. Either act is a violation against my Civil Rights. I've since received response letters from certain Government officials telling me that they cannot assist nor fund my Company's efforts to eliminate Poverty and homelessness in America. (Their Corresponded Letters is Included) Even though Congress and the Federal Reserve can't account for $8.5. to 12- Trillion dollars of Taxpayer's money that seemingly goes missing every 3- Years. And yet, since the 1990s to 2018, the Federal Reserve continues to allocate a never-ending yearly alleged military defense budget to the Pentagon of $630-Billion Dollars. The same amount of the funding request; outlined in KMRCDS Company's Plans.

I. Problem Statement

The Laws of the United State Senate Congress Assembled and the Board of Governors of the Federal Reserve System is dangerously affecting Myself, family members and everyone in America. The formal complaint is based on the Board of Governors of the Federal Reserve System, Congress Assembled, State Senate lack of empathy or attention to the ongoing problems of Poverty and Homelessness. It is contributed to the unethical and illegal Government Policy Laws that seem to be deliberate acts of Corruption and Abuse.

When all options have failed in acquiring assistance from local Government Corporate Business Services then it is the duties of the Funders who fund these Government Corporate Business Services. It is up to your office to step in to make sure that your Executive Branches is provided the assistance that is requested by its **Indigenous** Taxpayer. As it is written in the Constitution, Declaration and numerous Treaty Laws. The reason why Congress has a written Law was because of the continuous savage conflict between them, and the British Government in 1776-1785 Act. Unfortunately, their Foreign savage conflict has spilled over and illegally forced its unwarranted Law Policies unto the Indigenous Negro Americans way of life. As a result, today Tyranny Reign Supreme in America. And not one Indigenous Negro American ever signed an agreement or contract of compliance.

A new rule of Law was written on December 20, 2017, by President Donald Trump information are as follows;

December 20, 2017, President Donald J. Trump signed Executive Orders called "Executive Orders, Blocking the Property of **Foreign Persons** Involved in Serious Human Rights Abuse or Corruption" (The entire Presidential Executive Order document is attached to this Proposal) This order is pertaining to **"Any"** Foreign Government Organization that Presence themselves as a President of a Country, Senator, Congress, Council, Military or Police Enforcement, Government Funders and all its

Affiliates whom are working within the U.S. or Outside of the U.S. That have been Committing or is currently committing "<u>Severe Human Rights Abuse and Corruption against</u> "**Any**" Group or Individual (s) living in America. <u>Must be removed from their position of "**Any**" high ranking Office. Land, Properties, and Compensation Must be Rendered to the victims.</u>

The European Colonizers of the United States Congress Assembled established itself in the year 1790. According to the Census Bureau, thousands of Europeans started to arrive into this Country in record numbers from 1913-1940. Therefore, they couldn't possibly consider themselves as Indigenous to America. The substantial evidence that's outlined in K.M.R.C.E.D. Constitutional Law Decree suggests that the entire U.S. Government Federal Business Corporation is in fact, a "<u>Foreign</u>" European Government Business Corporate Entity". Its establishment was flat out refused and considered to be an illegal Crime against Humanity. Due to its direct inhumane actions to cause <u>Severe Human Rights Abuse and Corruption</u>" against the Indigenous Negros and/or African American Population. And just like any other Business Corporation within our society must be held accountable for their ongoing criminal actions of Bias intent. The U.S. Government has appointed itself "Responsible" As the People's Public Servants". Therefore, they are employed on Payroll" to address the most important issues that the American people are faced with today.

The Position and Duties held by United State Senate Congress Assembled;

U.S. Congress makes laws that influence our daily lives. It holds hearings to inform the legislative process, conducts investigations to oversee the Executive Branch, and is elected to Serve as the Voice of The People and the states in the federal government. Congress receives all taxpayers' monies to financially Support all governmental Branches and Public services that we see today. From the Public's Consumerism on everything that is produced on this planet. All its profits, Taxes, Insurances, capital are collected into the Board of Governors of the Federal Reserve System. In which they receive well over $3 Trillion each year. A small portion of that could easily eliminate Poverty and Homelessness. As a result, certain crimes in America would no longer exist.

United State Senate Congress, legislative, lawmaking, branches of the national government also share power with the President of the United State and the Supreme Court. The writers of the U.S. Constitution and Declaration thought Congress Assembled was so important, they listed it first! Congress has two parts, the Senate and the House of Representatives. Both must work together for the Wellbeing, Safety, Security, and Sustainability for the People as it is written in the Declaration and Constitution. And when all other Governmental entities have failed the People? The people must submit their written Grievances to U.S. Senate Congress Assembled. And if, the U.S. Congress refuses to accommodate its Constituents would be considered as Treason, Felony and a Breach of the Peace. And can be the subject of removal.

U.S. Government Veteran News Reporting

Aired on C-Span-3 News, in 2013 The Federal Reserve Inspector Coleman was held into questioning by the House of Representatives Alan Grayson about $8.5 Trillion suddenly came up missing claiming it has "Dodge an Audit" And prior to that on February of 2010 during the Bush administration according to (D) Florida Representative Alan Grayson $12- Trillion Dollars has come up missing. Veteran and Senior Editor of Todays Newspaper Gordon Duff explains "The Pentagon works much like the Federal Reserve, we have overt and co-overt policy's, we have so many un-necessary Black budget Project including nuclear weapons developments and huge overspending budgets as earlier as 1980's- 1991 as they continue to eat Tax Payers Money".

The Federal Reserve System collects Trillions of dollars each year through Taxes, Insurance, Consumerism and much more. As the People need a home it should not be looked upon as an Economic Consumerisms Opportunity" for the Federal Reserve to collect profits. A home is our #1 Necessity to our Survival. And with the amount of money being collected by the Federal Reserve System each year. No one especially the Indigenous population should Pay for their Own Basic Human Right's needs. This is considered an all-out Crime and a disgrace! It's literally a crime against humanity. For generations, people are doing just about "Anything" to obtain the U.S. Dollar in providing an important need for their basic survival. Just think of the amount of damage, stress and strain the Federal Reserve System and Congress has caused its own Citizens and the Indigenous. Just think what people can do and achieve if they were not illegally being forced to pay for housing Mortgage and Rental fees. Certain Crimes and Poverty would end an instant! The solution to this most egregious problem is fully explained in K.M.R.E.C.D.S. Company's Initiatives. Below is a brief outline of how the Federal Reserve operates its functions copied from its Official Website.

<u>This statement is on the Federal Reserve Broad Website states the Following:</u>

The Federal Reserve System is the central bank of the United States. It performs five general functions to promote the effective operation of the U.S. economy and, more generally, the public interest. The Federal Reserve *conducts the nation's monetary policy to promote maximum employment, stable prices, and moderate long-term interest rates in the U.S. economy; *promotes the stability of the financial system and seeks to minimize and contain systemic risks through active monitoring and engagement in the U.S. and abroad; *promotes the safety and soundness of individual financial institutions and monitors their impact on the financial system as a whole; *fosters payment and settlement system safety and efficiency through services to the banking industry and the U.S. government that facilitate U.S.-dollar transactions and payments; and *promotes consumer protection and community development through consumer-focused supervision and examination, research and analysis of emerging consumer issues and trends, <u>community economic development activities,</u> and the administration of consumer laws.

Funding Requirement Statement

The required Funding request would implement Katherine's Magical Revitalization Economic Community Development Initiatives and the Company's Constitutional Law Decree. Both must be approved as a Bill Act Law" of Great Urgency to ALL Americans who desperately need the services. The funding deliveries consist of the following;

The required Funding could come in 2 forms of payment or it could all be rendered as the total amount stated below. The First Initial request for the K.M.R.E.C.D. Promotional Headquarters Building" The total Start-up $178. Million outlined in the Company Business Plan.

The Additional Funding is noted herein;

<u>Total Funding:</u>

> ➢ Startup Costs for the State of California; $7- Billion Dollars. And additional capital fees of $7-Billion equals to $14-Billion Dollars.

- For 45 States, $7 Billion each equaling to $315 Billion Dollars+ additional capital fees of $315 Billion Dollars. Totaling to $630-Billion Dollars for the United States for 3-Years.
- The additional $7 Billion in capital fees for each State may not be requested due to the completion and satisfactory of the initially required state developments.

Additional U.S. Congress Bill Act Law Requirements

1. The U.S. Housing Cost market, in the Year 1618-1776 would be applied as the same purchasing housing cost for all INA and/or A.A. participating Clients. This is fully explained below.

2. Certificate of Safety and Protection, throughout the Lands of America for all INA and/or A.A. participating Clients.

3. Certificate of Land Business Development free from Taxations and Penalties for all INA and/or A.A. participating clients.

4. Vehicle: Tags, Registration and License fees are null and void for all INA and/or A.A. Participation Clients.

5. Insurance: If INA, A.A. clients are paying monthly Insurance on "ANYTHING" then that person must be paid back the full accumulated amount each year on the first of April.

6. Taxes: Whatever is purchased with a Tax must be paid back the full amount of those accumulated taxes each year on the first of April.

The Housing Deed Ownership Certificate is the fastest and simplest way to end poverty in America. If approved by Congress, State Senate, this will eradicate the threat of poverty and certain crimes to more than 80%. The economy would grow due to the population of more spending; more products and services would expand productivity would increase. People would worry less, working class would increase, new businesses would emerge due to individuals being able to own their home. People would be able to pay for more important things in life like Health care coverage, College tuition, Insurance, Pursuit of Happiness and Life would be more Prosperous and sustainable.

Today's High Cost of living

The average monthly cost for a decent Home in a great neighborhood in the State of California is $4,500 dollars and up. This does not include monthly utilities such as; Gas, Electricity, Water, Garbage, Phone and Internet equaling to $380,00. An average monthly food expense for a family of six is $850,00. And important other miscellaneous uses $350.00. Plus, savings $500.00 total to $6,580.00. Meanwhile, the average employment income is $900.00 to $2,000 per month. Therefore, the average person results to either living with Family, Friends, Roommates or the person is Homeless.

To eradicate the Poverty and Homeless problem

Based on the K.M.R.E.C.D.S. Community Policy Initiatives. The cost of a home of any size anywhere in America. Would be based on the cost of a home prior to the U.S. Congress Assembled Establishment in 1776-1785. Based on the year of 1618-1776 estimating value cost of would be implied to the cost of a home today in the year 2018-2019.

For example; When applying for housing at any one of the K.M.R.E.C.D.S Public Social Service assisted Programs. Clients from the starting age of 18 years old and up will be eligible to receive their "Housing Deed Ownership Certificate" at any one of our F.G.P.L.C. Banking Branch Offices. Indigenous clients will then take their "Housing Deed Certificate to any professional Real Estate Company in the U.S. to acquire a home of their choice according to the individual or family size. Once the Participant finds a home let's say in Malibu or Beverly Hills California. The Real Estate Agent will tally up the "Blue Book value" amount estimating of how much the house would've cost in 1618-1776. If, the house estimates to let's say Zero to $5,000 dollars?

Then that's how much the Indigenous client would pay for their home. Qualified customers would receive their Deed Certificate, Housing profile and Keys within 45 minutes of completing their 2 -page housing "Deed" Application. To achieve this, the K.M.R.E.C.D.S. Policy Plan may be presented through a Bill Act Policy Law of Great Urgency" and the Approval of Funding from the Federal Reserve Act. In the same importance matters of how other Government Corporate agencies are funded and implemented in our everyday society. Such as; The Federal Reserve System, the U.S. Prison/Jails Business Services, Internal Revenue Services, U.S. Medical Pharmaceutical Companies, the U.S. Pentagon.

(Sent to them by Certified Mail Dated: September 2013 and April 2018)

New Alternative Reparation Solution Plans, for African American BILL ACT

Testimony of

Ms. Katherine Irvin, Company Founder/CEO, and Author.

A representative of California in support of H.R. 40 Commission
To study and Approve of Reparation Solution
Plan for African American, Act.

Requesting Signing of BILL or Support for Proposal Plan Approval.
Submitted June 16, 2019

Hello and thank you for taking the time to review this most Important Alternative Reparation Solution Proposal. I am the Founder, CEO, and Manager of "S.S.H.E.A.- The Successful Service Housing and Educational Arena's, Inc" and the Founder, CEO of "K.M.I.R.E.D.S.- Katherine's Magical Inner-City Revitalization & Economic Development Service Inc". Both Companies are designed to eliminate Poverty, Homelessness, Racial injustices, Mass Incarceration, Crimes and much more. Our Company services are unlike any Urban Development and Social Service Welfare Group in the World. We would provide Nationwide Permanent Housing, Education & Business Opportunities for Economic Empowerment starting with the State of California. The Company would generate well over $ 1 Trillion Dollars in annual Sales, tremendous Economic Expansion Potential for the States is Assured! Our Company Service Policy is a great beneficial asset for All Americans of ALL Races, Colors, and Backgrounds.

This 16- page document outlines my Testimony, Experience and (3) various Reparation Solution Plans for review. This proposal gives a proper analysis of the true meaning of Reparations and provides a list the Current Problems stemming from the Atlantic Slave Trade. With a list of the greatest Solution for those Problems. It this proposal is approved; our Company services intend to transform and Revitalize Impoverished Urban Communities that will extend its gratitude and services for the Greater Good of All Humanity. After reviewing this Proposal BILL, please request for the full Project Development Plan and/or Business Plans that are outlined in this document. Thank you very much and I look forward to speaking with you all very soon!

Brief Background

I, Katherine Irvin, American Black -Negro Descendant. Born April 10, 1968, in Chicago IL. My Grand Parents on my Mother Side are Indigenous Negro's to Illinois, California, and Louisiana. and on my Father, the side we're Indigenous Negro's to Stillwater, Tulsa Oklahoma, and Texas. According to Congress, they would be considered as "Freed Negro Indians" Many Incidents stemming from the Atlantic Slave Trade have caused one of the most Heinous City Massacre in Human History. It took place in Tulsa Oklahoma on June 21, 1921. My Grand Parents initially planned on owning several Businesses in the Black Wall Street District; one business was farming and the other was the Food Market Store. They would tell us stories about how peaceful and prosperous it was prior to1921 Tulsa City Massacre. Several years prior to the Deadly Massacre White Negative Tension grew more intense. Then a sudden burst of violence gave way in the Town causing my grandparents to flee for their lives. My Grand Parents moved back to Stillwater just several miles over and never returned to Tulsa.

Years later the Oklahoma City of Urban & Renewal in 1937-1963 forced my Grandparents into court to take possession of our Land. The City took the land and because of that, my Grandparents could no longer financially sustain themselves. They later moved Northeast to Grand Rapids Michigan. This has cut off any links to our Legacy for Financial Sustainability. It severely altered and damaged their way of life causing them to live in poverty and shame, they were never able to recover from it. Now throughout our entire lives, my family and I are struggling through Homelessness and Poverty. Incidences like this are just one out of Millions across America. We were stripped -away from our Legacy & Identity causing generations to be plunged into a never-ending cycle of poverty and homelessness. It is the #1 root cause of Drug Abuse, Severe Mental Anguish, and Crimes. I don't just speak for myself I speak for all Indigenous Negro Americans and African Americans as well as white settlers and Hispanic Americans that were also victimized by the backlash stemming from Slavery in America.

Millions of wealthy and prosperous families were all destroyed by white settlers and/or of the U.S. Congress Assembled. Their ways of unleashing

Racial Terror and Land Property Theft left millions without homes. If it were not for the criminal acts held by Congress during the Enslavement to Emancipation Act in 1833 in Philadelphia. Millions of families including my own would've kept their Businesses going to its fullest potential. We would've expanded and prospered from our Legacy, opportunities and Prosperity would've been our normal way of life and I speak for Millions!

My goal is to one day receive the necessary funding to own my own Home with lots of Land to build a Large Food Garden and Animal Rescue Sanctuary. In a Prosperous Safe Community from my own Creative Development Skills.

Experience

Every race, culture or creed should already be made aware of by now of the fact, that during the era of 1619 the United States Government -Corporate Business, and its Executive Offices have greatly thrived and prospered from the Enslavement of the Negro Population. As a result, of their Corporate Policies being enforced is the #1 Cause of Most Problems that are occurring Today. Our Company is here to fix, re-arrange or eliminate those Problems.

Since 2007 I Katherine Irvin founded two companies called "S.S.H.E.A- Successful Service Housing & Educational Arena's Inc. and K.M.I.R.E.D.S.- Katherine's Magical Inner-City Revitalization & Economic Development Service Inc". I was never successful in getting my Company off the ground due to lack of Government Funding and Support.

Both Companies are designed to eliminate Poverty, Homelessness, and Crimes. By providing Community Revitalization services to transform Urban areas into what most people would call "Promise Land Styled Communities". We specialize in combing Extraordinary Theme Parks and Community Housing Together' This service also provides (3) of the Best Reparation Solution Plans in America! Written for the approval of the United States Senate, Local Legislation, Congress Assembled and the President of the United States.

Current Problem Statement

Since July of 2008 I've Presented my Companies "Business Plans" to former *President William Jefferson Clinton) *California Senator Dianne

Feinstein through April 2007-2018) *Congresswoman Maxine Waters 2010) President Barack Obama in 2009 – 2013) *California Governor Jerry Brown 2009 -2017) *Local Congressmen Paul Cook 2016) *Local Legislation Assembly 2015- 2017) *The Governors of the Federal Reserve System September 2018-2019) U.S. Department of Community Housing and Economic development January 2019) Small Business Administration March 2019.

All government officials have notified me, through letters of acknowledging and local business meetings. And all have rejected my idea suggesting that I apply for Government Grants and Banking Loans. I informed them all that it would be virtually impossible given the circumstances, in which their U.S. Policy Law is written and carried out. Like so; "In order to be granted any Government Grant, Banking Business loan or to receive funding from any Small Business Administration. These following credentials must be present during any Loan process.

- ✓ Half of the funds that are being requested must be in your Bank Account.
- ✓ Certain valuable Collateral must be added.
- ✓ The Business itself must be successfully operating 2- years prior.
- ✓ An Annual Tax fee of $873.00 dollars is required to own a Corporation.
- ✓ Must have a perfect credit score of 720-800
- ✓ Four References from successful Business Partnerships.

I've have informed them that their business loan policy requirements would be nearly impossible for an average impoverished person to achieve in starting a business. This is partly the reason why Only 3.8% of African Americans are business owners. No government official has given any response back to my return request. The non-compliance, bias complacency of the United States government officials must be addressed.

Why Should Congress or the U.S. President Approve American Reparations?

Because it's the Right thing to Do. Because criminal acts that were made by Congress in the Past continues to cost the lives of Millions in our Present time. Currently affecting our progress and way of life. And, despite the near annihilation of our Great, Great Grand Parents. Our Great Grandparents Did NOT sign any agreement or contract to allow their Bodies and their

Country to be taken over by Anyone other than themselves! We are their Descendants whether you call us African Americans or Indigenous Negro Americans doesn't manner because we're all being victimized till this very day. We are here to establish Prosperous, Safe and Sustainable Communities. That would've been implemented Centuries ago if it were not for the Foreign take-over and enslavement that began in 1619.

Unethical Assumptions;

The notion that only "Certain African Americans" can receive Reparations is ridiculous! Some have mentioned unrealistic theories that "Only those who can prove that their Great Grandparents were enslaved is completely unethical. Throughout history have shown two types of enslavement that took place in America during 1619-1865. There is overwhelming evidence that proves more than 50% of African Americans are in fact Indigenous to America. Congress Assembled has always been aware of that fact. According to U.S. Congress Archives and 1790 Census Bureau all Black Americans were called "Indians" from 1619-1950's, then "Freed Negro Indians" from the 1950-1970s, today were labeled as African Americans from the 1980's-2019. In My Authored Book "The Arrival of the Promise Land" shows slavery taking place on both sides of the enslavement era and is nevertheless entitled to Reparations. In which all that is written herein can be proven in an Open Public Court of Law.

Analytical Approach to the Solution of Reparations.

Our bases for Reparations are in terms of actual true evidence through extensive historical research, life experience, and Testimony from the current Oppressed Victims.

And, how the effects from the Slave Trade Act are negatively affecting people's lives today. Only then can Reparation- Compensation be applied through the instructional concepts of our Company's Constitutional Law Policy and Company Services.

When we think of Reparations the first thing that pops in everyone's mind is "40 Acres and a Mule" resulting in Millions of dollars being given to each Black American. But that is not what real Reparations are about. True Reparations for Indigenous Negro Americans and African Americans must be implied in terms of the kinds of Law Policies that were in place Prior to 1619-1865. I compiled the bases of the Original Humanity Policy Law of how people once lived thousands of years prior to 1619. Original Services and Opportunities that would've been implemented throughout America. And if we applied these Original Humanity Services in our today society would quickly lead to everlasting Prosperity, Safety and Sustainability whether your Black, White, Green or Purple.

In all Fairness in logical reasoning; "40 Acres and a Mule" today would consist of "Safety, Prosperity, Sustainability with Unlimited Opportunities" And we compiled them into three various Compensation Plans starting with the State of California and across America.

1. Reparation Housing Compensation BILL- Eliminating Poverty & Homelessness.
2. United States Law Policy Re-construction ACT- Eliminating Mass Incarceration, Police Brutality, Racial Injustices, and Government Corruption and Abuse.
3. $630 Billion Dollar Reparation BILL- Development of both Companies for America.

It's ideal to combine all three as the Greatest America Solution Plan Ever Created!

The Benefits of the New Alternative Reparation Solution Plan;

1. Poverty and Homelessness for ALL Americans would No Longer Exist.
2. 90% decrease in Theft, Domestic Violence, Mental Stress, and Anguish.
3. 90% decrease in Gang Violence, Mass Incarceration, and Police Brutality.
4. An annual $1 Trillion Dollar boost into the American Economy structure.
5. Unlimited Opportunities and Enrichment Services for ALL People of ALL Races.

Reparation Compensation BILL ACT 1, 2 and 3
Eliminating Poverty, Homelessness, and Crime in an Instant!

Housing and Transportation Reparation Compensation BILL #1

We refer to our Clients as; A.A.R.C.-African American Reparation Clients and I.N.A.R.C. Indigenous Negro American Reparation Clients. The Successful Service Educational Training Programs provides I.N.A.R.C. and A.A.R.C. with the option to apply for Education & Career Training Services and/or apply for Housing and Vehicle Ownership Certificates. That allows a person to purchase a Home, Land or Vehicle at the cost value rate as if the year was 1618. Prior to the Atlantic Slave Trade in 1619.

For example; We accept Housing & Transportation Applicants at the starting age of 16 years old at any one of our S.S.H.E.A. Office Locations. A qualified Reparation Client could also apply for Emergency Financial Assistance, Education, Career and Business Training. For babies receiving their birth certificate will have a Secured notice of agreement for the "Housing and Transportation Compensation Entitlement" written on the back of their Birth Certificate. And whenever that individual turns 16 or 18 years of age old he or she will have the opportunity to receive home and transportation service according to their immediate situation and need Most Underage children and teenagers who acquire a home. Will be encouraged to live at any one of our Successful Service Housing & Educational Arena Facilities.

The Housing Deed Ownership Certificate is the fastest and simplest way to end poverty in America. If approved by President Trump this will instantly eliminate poverty, homelessness, and crime across America starting with California State. Millions of families and individual will be suddenly relieved and rid of severe mental stress and depression. Millions of people who are employed will have the opportunity to spend their hard-earned money on important things that matters the most. The economy would grow tremendously due to more spending; more productivity, Business services, and Job increase are assured. This is just a small example of the possibilities of this unique Reparation Solution Plan.

Here's how it works;

INA and A.A. Reparation Clients will be referred over to the office of (S.S.E.T P) Successful Service Educational Training Program. Here is where they'll apply for their Housing and Transportation Deed Application. They can also apply for Education and Career Training to gain the skills necessary for the development of our services. Once the application is received it could take anywhere from 15 Minutes to 2-days for their Housing Certificate. Once they receive their Housing and Transportation Certificate. Clients will then call or report to their local Real Estate Agent Company anywhere in the U.S. They would give their Housing Certificate to the Real Estate agent to acquire a home of their choice. Their Housing Compensation would be appropriate to fit their individual or family size. Once the Participant finds a home that's for sale let's say in Malibu or Beverly Hills California. The Real Estate Agent will tally up the "Blue Book value" amount estimating of how much the house would've cost in 1618. If, the house estimates to let's say Zero to 5,000 dollars? Then that's how much the INA and A.A. Client would pay for that Home or Vehicle.

Qualified Reparation customers would receive their Deed Certificate, Housing profile and Keys within 45 minutes of completing their 2 -page housing "Deed" Application. This Reparation Housing Plan is considered of Great Urgency" In the same way governments are funded and implemented in our everyday society. Such as; The Federal Reserve Banking System, the Pentagon Military, U.S. Prison/Jails Business Services, Internal Revenue Services, U.S. Medical Pharmaceutical Companies, etc. These government services have already been funded it's now time for a New Reparation Solution BILL to be funded.

<u>United States Law Policy Re-Construction BILL ACT #2</u>

This service eliminates Police Brutality, Government Injustices, Mass Incarceration, and Severe Mental Stress, Strain and Depression. We will work with Law Makers in Congress to eliminate "Certain" Law Policies that are listed below. Are completely Unwarranted and Goes against the Gian of all Humanity. Success is assured if funding support is approved. For the development of our Public Social Service Department. I.N.A and A.A. Reparation Clients could apply for the following services;

- ➢ Certificate of Safety and Protection throughout the Lands of America for all INA and A.A. participating Clients.
- ➢ Birth Certificate each Negro Person born in America must have their Legacy Rights of "Home & Development" written on the back of their Birth Certificate.

- Certificate of Business Funding and Development free from Taxations and Penalties for all INA and A.A. participating clients.
- Vehicle: Tags, Registration and License fees are null and void for all INA and A.A. Participation Clients.
- Insurance: Monthly Insurance payments on "ANYTHING" must be paid back the full accumulated amount every year on April 1st.
- Internal Revenue Taxes: Whatever is purchased with a Tax must be paid back their full amount of accumulated taxes each year on April 1st

$630 Billion Dollar Reparation BILL IDEA #3

Funding request for the Company's Development of; S.S.H.E.A. Successful Service Housing & Educational Arena's Inc. and K. M.I.R.E.D.S. Katherine's Magical Inner-City Revitalization Economic Development Service Inc. Serving every State in America.

- Startup Costs for the State of California; $7- Billion Dollars. An additional back up $7-Billion equals to 14-Billion Dollars for a possible 2-years.
- For 45 States, $7 Billion Dollars each equaling to $315 Billion Dollars, additional capital fees of 315 Billion Dollars. Total $630-Billion Dollars for 3-Years.
Totaling to $1.8 Trillion Dollars.

The additional $7 Billion for each State may or may not be requested due to the completion and satisfactory of all required state Company developments.

This Reparation Solution Plan must be approved based on the following facts:

- ❖ Unpaid Forced Slaved Wages must be paid to the Descendants, Ancient Artifacts, Land, Home, and Business Theft must be returned to the Rightful Heirs, Compensation for the vicious murder of our Great Grandparents is still unpaid.
- ❖ This Country has always been equally shared by various Tribe populations prior to the existence of the European race. Therefore, no foreign Government has the right to force its Laws upon another race of People.

- In 1619 through 2019, not one Indigenous Negro American, African Americans nor Native Americans have ever signed any contract or agreement with Congress Assembled that would allow them to take over our Country that was Never given to them.
- The United States Government in Congress Assembled must attempt to repair the devastating damage that is caused by their <u>Corporation Business Law Practices</u>.
- This Reparation Solution plan is long overdue and would've already been established today had it not been for the Atlantic Slave Trade Act. Formed by U.S. Congress.

The following is a brief look at the Company services for Community Revitalization, Economic Empowerment and Sustainability for generations.

Katherine's Magical Revitalization Economic Community Development Service.

Indigenous Negro Constitutional Law Decree

Introduction

This Indigenous Law Decree is written on June 6, 2013, by Ms. Katherine Irvin Founder/CEO, President

"I Katherine Irvin, Indigenous Negro American hereby formed this Constitutional Law Decree and its Current and Historical Fact Statement. Based on State of Emergency written Policy Law. For the Safety, Wellbeing, Stability, Livelihood, and Happiness for all Indigenous Negroes Americans and African American population. Establishing the Law, Policy's, Requests and Regulations of our Company is by way of Human Right, Sovereignty within all Indigenous Lands of America. This Decree is Ordained for the living rights of All Indigenous Negroes American Population.

We, DECLARE, we are the direct Bloodline Descendants too the Ancient Olmec's of America, Queen Califia of the California Blacks and many, many other Black, Brown, Copper Colored Native Tribes living throughout our American Lands. Certain Land right areas throughout America, Financial Compensation, Housing Ownership Policy Laws and Business Ventures must be granted for the development of Katherine's Magical Revitalization Economic Community Development Services Inc.

We are Indigenous. We are Sovereign. And yet, our very lives have always been under Constant threat by a Foreign Government Business Corporation of the 13 Colonies. Since 1776 establishment our Great Grandparents State Lands, Rivers and Seas, Valuable Possessions, Heirlooms, Resources, and Identity were illegally confiscated and must be returned to the rightful heirs of the Indigenous. The unwarranted acts of unimaginable malicious and destruction have caused ongoing acts of Government Corruption and Severe Human Rights Abuse till this very day in 2019.

Katherine's Magical Constitutional Law Decree is here to Correct the Wrong, to establish Communities of Safety, Economic Prosperity, and Sustainability. While spreading Good Well towards all people of all Races and Nationalities.

INA and A.A. mean Indigenous Negro American and African Americans.

K.M.R.C.E.D.S INDIGENOUS CONSTITUTIONAL
HUMAN RIGHTS LAW DECREE.

Section -A

I. The Company of Katherine's Magical Revitalization Economic Community Development Service will be developed based on how societies would've been like today if the establishment of the U.S. Government Business Corporation never took place in America. The Company's services are morally based on the type of Public Social Services and Business Enterprises that would've been implemented into our society today if America was never colonized and destroyed.

2. No Indigenous Negro American nor African Americans have "NEVER" signed any written contract agreement with any of the U.S. Department Government Business Corporation, that was established in 1790 according to the Census Bureau. There was "NEVER" a contract agreement in which the foreign Europeans/Jewish/Arab had the right to rule, dictate or govern over another.

3. No Foreign Government and its Affiliations has the right to go against an Indigenous Person's Free Will, Life- long Liberty and Happiness. This is the bases for our written Law Decree. Therefore, "ANY" type of Severe Human Rights Abuse against the Indigenous People of their Lands and of their way of life. Must remove themselves from their current Positions, Land Property and Compensation must be rendered to the Indigenous victims. The order of Authority is in the hands of the Indigenous appointee and must be Highly Honored and Respected as Sovereign Law.

4. As it is also written on December 20, 2017, Executive Orders, Blocking the Property of <u>Foreign Persons</u> Involved in Serious Human Rights Abuse or Corruption. If ANY U.S. Government Employee Officials feels upset, uncomfortable or angry over what is written? Understand that "Everything that is Written Herein is the Absolute Truth. All evidence can be presented and proven in an <u>Open Public Court of Law!</u>

<u>The United States Executive Order Statement</u>

On December 20, 2017, President Donald J. Trump signed an Executive Order called "Executive Orders, Blocking the Property of <u>Foreign Persons</u> Involved in Serious Human Rights Abuse or Corruption" (The entire Presidential Executive Order document is attached to this Proposal) This order is pertaining to "Any" Foreign Government Organization that Presence themselves as a President of a Country, Senator, Congress, Council, Military or Police Enforcement and all its Affiliates whom are working within the U.S. or Outside of the U.S.

That has been Committing or is currently committing "Severe Human Rights Abuse and Corruption against "Any" Group or Individual (s) living in America. Must be removed from their position of "Any" high ranking Office. And Land, Properties and Compensation Must be Rendered back to the victims. President Donald J. Trump added a list of Presidents from other Countries but failed to add themselves on the Annex List of "Foreign" Corrupt government entities operating in America.

5. The European Colonizers of the United States Congress Assembled established itself in the year 1790. According to the Census Bureau, thousands of Europeans started to arrive into this Country in mass numbers in 1913-1940. Therefore, they couldn't possibly consider themselves as Indigenous to America. The substantial evidence that's outlined in KMK Sovereign Constitutional Law Decree suggests that the entire U.S. Government Federal Business Corporation is in fact, a "Foreign" European Government Business Corporation Entity." Its establishment was flat out refused and considered to be a crime against Humanity.

6. Due to its direct inhumane actions to cause Severe Human Rights Abuse and Corruption" against the Indigenous Negros and African American Population. And just like any other Business Corporation within our society must be held accountable for their ongoing criminal actions of Bias intent. The U.S. Government has appointed itself "Responsible" As the People's Public Servants." Therefore, they are employed on Payroll" to address the most important issues that the American people are faced with today.

*The Company of K.M.E.C.D.S. is written and formed by Ms. Katherine Irvin. A Sovereign Indigenous Negro American. Our Company comes with its own Indigenous Sovereign Constitutional Law Decree. The instructional Law Policies, Rules, Financial Requests and Regulations as it is written must be admitted, abide granted and highly respected. By the Foreign United States President, Vice President and Congress Assembled.

The U.S. President December 20th Executive Orders would positively affect the decisions of approval to the KMK Company's Financial Request, Policies, Rules, and Regulations. Based on The U.S. President December 20th Executive Orders written terms of being a "Foreign" Business Corporation entity themselves. And can be easily proven in an "Open Public Court of Law."

Section- B

I. The United States Government Business Corporation, Duns # 052714196

Must Respect the Written Laws, Rules, Policies, Boundaries from the K.M.R.E.C.D. Company's Law Decree of which it Stands. The United State Foreign Government Congress Assembled must conduct the most positive and effective measures to correct the wrong that has been done to the Indigenous Negro Americans, African American People. These U.S. Government entities listed below Must make the necessary compensation towards what is written herein. "Certain" Amount of Land with Rivers, Lakes, Oceans {Per State} must be divide accordingly throughout the Lands of America and aboard.

II. Any European Foreigner of any descendants living in America or abroad Cannot imply or enforce any of its laws, rules or regulations upon the Indigenous Negro and African American People within their own lands, nor upon the Wildlife Animal and its forestry lands. To enforce any foreign Law policy against another is, in fact, a criminal act against their Civil Sovereign Rights. The Divine Sovereign Order did not give Any Authoritative rights to Any U.S government official. And if they cannot comprehend or if they disagree with what is written here? They will then be labeled as Criminally insane. In which they are always obligated to go back to their native homeland of Hell-Sinki Russia.

III. The following list below is the list of the Unauthorized Foreign U.S. Government Corporation Entities and their Dun's numbers in which their Laws, Regulations, and policies must automatically become Null and Void against all Indigenous Negro Americans and African American population. The U.S. Government such as; the FBI, CIA, DEA, Police Departments, Congress Assembled, Supreme Court Justice, Attorney General, and all other U.S. Branches Cannot take any Kind of Negative actions or Malicious Attacks and Deceptive measures or any arrest against the Indigenous Company Owner, Residents, Land developments on Land, Sea, Rivers, Lake and Air, Employees, Staff, Students, Members, Customers, Funders, Investors, Contractors, Companies for hire or Tourists. Shall Not Be Intimidated nor Harmed in any way.

Section III-A

United States Government-052714196
US Department of Defense (DOD)-030421397
US Department of Justice (DOJ)-011669674
US Department of State-026276622
US Department of Health & Human Services (HHS)-
Office of the Secretary-112463521
US Department of Education-944419592
US Department of Energy-932010320
US Department of Homeland Security-932394187

US Department of the Interior-020949010
US Transportation Security Administration (TSA)-050297655
US Federal Aviation Administration (FAA)-056622429
Bureau of Customs & Border Protection (CBP)-796730922
Federal Bureau of Immigration & Customs Enforcement (ICE)-130221646
US Environmental Protection Agency (EPA)-057944910
US Public Health Service (USPHS)-039294216
National Institutes of Health (NIH)-061232000
US Centers for Disease Control & Prevention (CDC)-927645465
US Food & Drug Administration (FDA)-138182175
US Internal Revenue Service (IRS)-040539587
Federal Reserve Board of Governors (Fed)-001959410
Federal Bureau of Investigation (FBI)-878865674
National Security Agency (NSA)-617395215
US Drug Enforcement Administration (DEA)-167247027
Federal Bureau of Alcohol, Firearms & Tobacco (BAFT)-132282310
Federal Bureau of Land Management (BLM)-926038563
United Nations (UN)-824777304

Section-C

IV.

Indigenous Human Right Emergency Funding Policy Law.

The ideal Financial Compensation Funding is $1.8 Trillion U.S. Dollars to be forwarded into the Financial Gold Protection Law Banking Branch.

Total Funding Requirements:

- Startup Costs for the State of California; $7- Billion Dollars. An additional capital fee of $7-Billion equals to 14-Billion Dollars.
- For 45 States, $7 Billion each equaling to 315 Billion Dollars + additional capital fees of 315 Billion Dollars. Total $630- Billion Dollars for 3-Years.
- The additional $7 Billion for each State may or may not be requested due to the completion and satisfactory of all required state developments.

Additional U.S. Government Requirements:

- **U.S. Housing Cost** in the Year 1618 would be applied as the same housing cost for all INA and A.A. Population. This is explained Below.
- **Certificate of Safety and Protection** throughout the Lands of America for all INA and A.A. participating clients.
- **Certificate of Business Development** free from Taxations and Penalties for all INA and A.A. participating clients.
- **Vehicle:** Tags, Registration and License fees are null and void for all INA and A.A. Participation clients.
- **Insurance:** If any INA, A.A. client is paying monthly Insurance fees on "ANYTHING" then that person must be paid back the full accumulated amount each year on April 1st.
- **Taxes:** Whatever is purchased with a Tax must be paid back the full amount of those accumulated taxes each year on April 1st.

Additional Required Funding Regarding Stolen Property and Valuable Possessions

Our Ancient artifacts and materials from the past will speak volumes to those who have returned. All Ancient Artifacts will be promptly displayed for all to see what life was like some millions of years prior. All stolen Ancient Ancestry Artifacts, materials, clothing items, and writings will come from various European museums like the Smithsonian, British, France, top floor and basement levels and private homes. These items that are currently stolen must be returned to the rightful Descendants of the Indigenous Negro Population and place carefully into our Magical Ancient Museum. Our Museum will be located wherever the Place of Dreams Theme Parks are at. This unique service gives the long-awaited its final resting place. Members will receive a historical connection, education, and inside information and great knowledge. More details of this Extraordinary Museum will be forth coming.

Additional Required Funding Regarding; Housing Deed Ownership Certificate.

The Housing Deed Ownership Certificate is the fastest and simplest way to end poverty in America. Congress, State Senate must approve this BILL. This will eradicate the threat of poverty and certain crimes to more than 80%. The economy would grow due to the population of more spending; more products and services would expand productivity received.

Participating clients of the "K.M.R.C.D.S will receive their Housing Deed Ownership Certificate" at any one of our participating F.G.P.L.C. Banking Branch Offices. Indigenous clients will then take their Housing Deed Certificate to any professional Real Estate Company in the U.S. To acquire a home of their choice in "ANY" State, City area according to the individual or family size. Once the Participant finds a home let's say in Malibu or Beverly Hills California. The Real Estate Agent will tally up the "Blue Book value" amount estimating of how much the house would've cost in 1618-1776. If, the house estimates to let's say Zero to 5,000 dollars?

Then that's how much the Indigenous client would pay for their home. Qualified customers would receive their Deed Certificate, Housing profile and Keys within 45 minutes of completing their 2-page housing "Deed" Application. To achieve this, the K.M.R.C.D.S Policy Plan may be presented through a Bill Act Policy Law of Great Urgency" and the Approval of Funding from the Federal Reserve Act. In the same importance matters of how other Government Corporate agencies are funded and implemented in our everyday society. Such as; The Federal Reserve System that fund such corporations like the U.S. Prison/Jails Business Services, Internal Revenue Services, U.S. Medical Pharmaceutical Companies, the U.S. Pentagon military services, homeland security, the police departments and more.

V. Regarding funding approval for this Company: It is not required for the Founder/CEO to provide a High-Ranking License, Diploma, Degree from a School, University/College. Neither to provide voting pole of signatures from the people as a petition for Congress and State Legislations. To decide on what the obvious decision should be. To suggest such an act would be unethical and irrelevant to the request from the Indigenous Founder. The relevant unanimous decision of a voting agreement depends on after the developments of our Company is established of satisfied, happy living residents participating in Katherine's Magical Revitalization Communities is equivalent to relevant Votes.

Section-D

VI. The worst thing you can do to a bird is to clip its wings and stick it in a birdcage. The worst thing you could do to any animal is to take it out of its natural habitat and keep it in a cage for human entertainment purposes. Imprisoning Animals in Public or Private Zoo's, Pet Stores, Carnivals or Circuses is against our Law Policies. Animals and Birds cannot speak out to let you know it doesn't want to be displayed. The Animal's Rights must be Respected and removed from any and all public and private Zoo's stores etc. and placed within Katherine's Magical Wildlife Sanctuary. Our Sanctuary is wherever Animal and Birds Previous lived.

VII. For funding approval of this Company; It is not required for the Founder/ CEO to provide a High- Ranking License, Diploma, Degree from a School, University/College. Neither to provide voting pole of signatures from the people as a petition for Congress and State Legislations. To decide on what the obvious decision should be. To suggest such an act would be unethical and irrelevant to the request from the Indigenous Founder. The relevant unanimous decision of a voting agreement depends on after the developments of our Company is established of satisfied, happy living residents participating in Katherine's Magical Revitalization Communities is equivalent to relevant Votes.

Section-E

VIII. We do not accept anyone into our Communities who would be considered mentally insane. The insanity that we speak of comes in many different categories such as, those who are obsessed with Any Kind of Religion, Pedophilia, Cults, Psychopathic behaviors, the Abuse and control over Men, Women, and Children. Killing and Capturing of Animals, obsessed with Guns, Bombs and destructive Weaponry, Constance thinking of deception, malice, hatred Murder, and negativity. If any person shows or who cannot be cured this type of thinking are forbidden from entering the Promise Land Community.

IX. An individual of ANY Race, Color, Nationality, and Culture are welcome to live in Katherine's Magical Residential Communities if he or she shows themselves of having Compassion, Respect, Kindness, Understanding, Morality Towards All Others are welcomed, of course, we are not all perfect, but you get the picture.

<u>Rules, Law Policy's and Regulations Regarding</u> Section III-A

X. Again, No Indigenous Person of America has ever signed any kind of Contract agreement with the U.S. European Colonizers to give rulership, authority, and dictatorship overall population. The U.S. Government Congress Assembled and all its federally funded Executive Branches are NOT Indigenous to America and are in fact, Foreign Entities Illegally

Operating itself on Occupied Stolen Land. Therefore, NO Police or Military forces of any European, Russian, Arab, Asian, Canadian, British, United States Government Can ever enter our Lands without full permission of the Residents. Absolutely NO entity of any kind whether it be their Justice Courts, Attorneys, Judges, Congress, Banks, United Nations Staff, ALL its Executive Branches, the CIA, the FBI, the MI6, their Special Intelligence branches, Private Militia groups, Bounty hunters, Homeland Security, IRS, Police Departments, Sheriff's Department, NRA Groups, U.S. Military, Navy, Army, Marines "Cannot" access any parts of Katherine's Magical Residential Communities and Business Service Lands, Sea and Air.

Communication is done only by way of Internet, Email, Fax or Phone. Postal Mail can only be done outside of all K.M.R.E.C.D.S. Communities areas. For safety precautions only. All Residents of S.S.H.E.A. Communities are free to come and go as they please but are forbidden to bring in groups that are listed herein unless most of the residents' grants permission. The reason why this must be is due to the fact those who are listed as (III-A) are NOT Indigenous to America. And have caused overwhelming destruction to the Indigenous Negro American Population. To the point that this Law Decree must be made and granted into Law for the people's own protection from Tyranny. With overwhelming prove that can be Presented in an "<u>Open Public Court of Law.</u>"

Section-F

XI. Katherine's Magical Residential Community" is to be developed, maintained secured by our finest Employees, Students-Graduates of many Trades called "The Successful Service Superhero's." They are the Graduates from the Successful Service Training Programs that are located inside every S.S.H.E.A. Facility. These individuals have the same Authoritative rights as any Police Officer, Judge, Lawyer, and Military Officer" and will uphold the law according to the law that is written herein, written the F.G.P.L. Banking Branch.

XII. Regarding Free, Free, Free! When the Indigenous Negro applies to become a Resident or either a Student, Employee of K.M.R.C.D. Community. They are applying to get business and career training to successfully operate and maintain the Company Lands, Residents, Services, Laws, Policy and Regulations, etc. By working together to whatever it is you like doing regarding the development of the Company. Will allow All Goods and Services to be used as FREE Services! For the residents, members, and students and are not limited to the following: Free Food, Retail, Appliance Stores, Medical/Dental, etc. Applicants will automatically receive the Deed to your Home that comes with their own Personalized Transportation. They are also provided with Free Education and Training towards the development and maintaining of their own Promise Land Community located throughout every City, State in America and Possibly the World.

Financial Payouts comes in the form of Gold tablets and Bullions, precious Medals that can be turned into U.S. Dollars or any type of Currency of that Country.

Section- G

XIII. We welcome all people from all Races, Ages, Colors, backgrounds to Enjoy themselves at any one of our Amazing Public Theme Park Service Attractions and Public Business Services that are mentioned in our Project Development plans and Website.

XIV Forbidden Deceptive Acts

1.) No outside Group or inside Company Business employee that we hire, nor students, Residents, Staff Members can ever harm anyone by way of physical violence, malice deception, or misleading acts. If a person cannot control their negative urges than they will be directed to the Therapy and counseling center. If a person physically warms or murders another person based on their negative urges and not from self-defense reasons? Then that person will be sent to our quarantine units for further evaluation and/ or transfer out of Company Areas. Directing them back into the European United State Government Society from which they came.

2.) If a worst-case scenario ever occurred. (God forbids!) Example: If a Staff Member, Student or Resident from our Company Services, suddenly loses their mind and goes outside of our Promise Land Community and Kills another Citizen. Then attempts to run back into our Community for refuge. The U.S. Police or Military cannot step one foot anywhere near our Community Areas to attempt to Retrieve the Suspect. Even if the entire incident was caught on camera, they could not enter the Company Areas under any circumstances. First, an immediate investigation will be conducted by Katherine's Investigation/ Legal Team. Everything must be thoroughly analyzed because we do not know whether the suspect was paid and hired by the U.S. Government CIA, FBI to do the unthinkable. For the sole purpose of the U.S. Police dept. To have an excuse to bombard they're way into Our Community to retrieve the fake suspect. Which would cause even more destruction then it already is. We will do an investigation to determine the situation.

3.) If the evidence shows, that suspect was indeed hired by the U.S. Government to do the unthinkable? Then we will quickly return him or her back into the hands of the U.S. Government. With a full public exposure detailing the entire incident through the People's Hall of Justice Court Media Network. However, if the Suspect was not involved with a Government plot? Then our Public Justice Law Courts will decide on his or her sentencing within our Quarantine Holding Facility. The U.S. Government cannot take any further actions against the K.M.R.C.D on the bases that they are NOT Indigenous to America. And cannot make any decisions on things that are out of our control. And if the government is feeling any kind of way about it, they can always return themselves back to their Bloodline native homeland in Helsinki of Russia.

Section-H

The Founder and President Ms. Katherine Irvin Specialize in the developments of the New Promise Land Styled Communities. Designed to change the world for the better. 99% of the people population will refer to our Communities as:

"The Promise Land- Meets Theme Park Heaven."

This Agreement of Partnership between all Indigenous Negro Americans and the Indigenous surrounding Continental Populations shall be binding upon the Respective Heirs, Executors, Administrators, Personal Representatives and of the Partners we chose. And as always times are forever changing. And, so can this Law Decree, it can change as needed according to the Natural Positive Order of things that are extremely Good and Healthy for a Happy, Prosperous, Sustainable Life forever and ever!

An Introduction to the Promise Land Company Public Social Services

- ❖ <u>Katherine's Magical Revitalization Economic Development Services</u>,

Housing and Business development service throughout America and abroad.

- ❖ <u>Successful Service Training Programs</u>, Provides Education, Career, and business training Courses for the Management of all services within Katherine's Magical Revitalization Community & Economic Development.
- ❖ <u>S.S.H.E.A.</u> is the home of the Successful Service Training Program Students. We house the impoverished, incarcerated, Neglected, Gangs, Homeless, Job Seekers, Struggling Families, Foster Children, Teens, etc.
- ❖ <u>Financial Gold Protection Law Card and Banking Institution</u>) Our Banking Branch Service Provide Gold Financial Assistance, Safety & Protection Service and Legal Assistance for Student Member Cardholders. Per-Paid Card Service for Tourist worldwide to enjoy any one of our Theme Park Services.
- ❖ <u>Safety Protection Services</u>) we provide monitoring secured protection services for all S.S.H.E.A. Residents, Students, Employees throughout America.

K.M.R.C.D.S-Business Services

- <u>Gold Mining Prospect Services</u> Gold mining Service, Providing Gold Payouts to Student members, Residents, Companies, Investors, etc.
- <u>The People's Hall of Justice Media Courthouse Network</u>
  "We the People" Public Media Legal services for Fair and Accurate accountability and Justice for all Races, Colors, Creeds and Nature Animals alike.

- <u>S.S.H.E. A #7</u> All-in-One Housing, Amusement Faculty.
- <u>The Place of Dreams</u> is the Largest Theme Park(s) in the World! Two would be placed in almost every State across America and abroad. For pure enjoyment, exploration and tremendous Economic Empowerment and Expansion.
- <u>Katherine's Magical Paradise Cruise Ship Travels</u>

Tourist and the public would be amazed at this One-of-A-Kind Domestic/International Travel service.

- <u>Katherine's Magical Ancient Museum</u>. Its where the Ancients come to Life!
- <u>Katherine's Magical Nature Animal Sanctuary</u>. We protect and cater to Nature wildlife, Birds, Creatures and Animals alike

The Company

This book provides the basic strategic information necessary for initial establishment and operation of (S.S.H.E.A.) Successful Service, Housing & Educational Arena's Inc. This document outlines the tactics for business growth, methods, procedures for operation, and infrastructure management.

(S.S.H.E.A' S.) Successful Service Housing & Educational Arenas, Inc are based on community revitalization, transforming all inner-city communities into safe, middle to Upper middle- class standards of living. Our services are geared towards Individuals and Family Participation in Community Reconstruction for Economic Empowerment and Sustainability.

We specialize in Prison Reform, Eliminating Gang violence, Homelessness, and Poverty. By providing unique enrichment programs, basic to college-level education, career training programs, emergency financial assistance and unique transitional housing to permanent housing services. For all ages, races, color or creed, in areas where the poverty rate is at 99%. S.S.H.E.A facilities are just one of our most popular and innovative community development services. It consists of an actual Stadium Dome Arena that's uniquely converted into a six-story "All-in-one" VIP apartment homes, school dormitory units with various Theme Park/ amusement services combined. For convenience, comfort, safety, education, and enjoyment. There are five distinct S.S.H.E.A. facilities. Each of them is geared towards individual needs, community transformation, participation in safety, education and overall economic expansion.

Financial Considerations

The marketing research and tailored marking strategy described in this business plan will result in after-tax profits at the lowest rate of $140,802,842 in year one, increasing to nearly $352,736,474 in after-tax profits within five years. It is estimated that by the year 2020, revenues will reflect a 1% market share in this industry in California. Monthly break-even stands at $3,214,236. Average Percent Variable Cost is around 64%.

Objectives

1. Earn sales of at least $ 725,370,000 in year one $1,504,127,232 by year two.
2. Obtain a gross margin higher than 36%
3. Achieve a net income of more than 19% of sales by the second year
4. The lowest profit sales estimate per city-state!

Mission Statement

(S.S.H.E.A.) the Successful Service Housing Educational Arenas Inc. Our mission of eliminating Homelessness, Poverty and Crime will ultimately, change the way government housing and welfare programs are currently being conducted. We plan on working with the County City and, State agencies to help improve their public social services. The implementation of our life-changing services will help eliminate the problems that exist in the following:

1. Ending Homelessness by 90%
2. Poverty will seize to exist.
3. Neighborhood Robberies, Home Invasion, and Thief will end by 90%
4. Gang Violence will seize to exist.
5. Mass Incarceration will seize to exist.
6. Un-Employment, Lack of Education will be obsolete.

[Keys to Success]

S.S.H.E.A. keys to success include but are not limited to the following:

1. Unique Method, Layout, and Concepts

2. Providing the most sought-after Housing, Business Services in the World.
3. Strong cross-promotional bases, between other affiliate organizations.
4. The Successful Service Training Programs.
5. Low cost admissions & transportation services.
6. Providing millions of new jobs per state.
7. Eliminating Gang Violence, Poverty and Homelessness

[Important Assumptions]

All financial projections and estimates are based on the following assumptions:

1. All services will continue to grow & receive the same success if not more.
2. This community development service will maintain its popularity, especially in major city areas nationally and possibly around the world.
3. Through new marketing techniques, the business will develop higher sales growth and tremendous worldwide notoriety.
4. Occupancy rates will average more than 40% throughout the year.
5. 3- months prior to the company's grand openings will Air our Major Motion Picture Film "The Arrival of the Promise Land" in Theaters worldwide.
6. This Movie/Film and our unique concept and layout will attract every Man, Women, and Child to our Company services Guaranteed!

The Golden Ticket Registration and Entrance Form

To become a student member of (S.S.H.E.A) Each person must be interviewed and mentally evaluated. So, that we may refer individuals and families over to their proper goal request. Interviews and evaluation will be conducted in a similar manner as a City Job interview. Potentials will not be turned away because of criminal classification, parole or felony status. Unless he or she is indicated on Police charts, Court Case records as having severe mental issues, violent, psychopathic and pedophile tendencies. Those individuals will not be able to qualify for any of our Services. However, we will work with the judicial system to obtain authorization to reopen certain closed cases associated with inmates that may be falsely accused, minor charges and or imprisoned unfairly.

Once the individual fills out their **"Golden Ticket Application".** Indicating the person living situation, household needs, goals, and ambitions. They will then receive their Personalized (F.G.P.L.C.) Financial Gold Protection Law Card. Uniforms, Trade School supplies. They will then be given a counselor and/or Mentor that will assign them to their dormitory housing unit of S.S.H.E.A.

With classrooms assignments into the Successful Service Training Programs.

There are seven levels of completion that must be actively applied in order to move forward onto higher levels of the program such as: (S.S.H.E.A.-7) for starters. A person can graduate from the Successful Service Training programs level 1 thru 7 within 6 months to 17 years depending on the age and Comprehension level of the individual. The main goal of our educational training program is to turn impoverished, neglected and confused individuals into successful service members of their communities. Students obtaining skills to become Professionals to society and their communities as professional Mentors, Teachers, Guardians, Community workers, safety leaders, engineers, construction developer, etc.

Problem #1 Homelessness, Crimes, Gang Violence, Mass incarceration, Lack of Education, Therapy/Counseling and Guidance.

Solution #1 Successful Service Educational Training Programs.

The company cannot exist without the (S.S.E.T.P) Successful Service Education

Training Programs. Revitalizing a community without Revitalizing the minds of the residents would be a failure and a waste of time and money. The S.S.E.T.P Successful Service Education Training Programs provides counseling and therapy, enrichment programs, basic level to college level Education, over 100 hands-on career training and business development opportunities and Gang suppression services. (S.S.E.T.P) would be implemented in every inner-city community throughout America. Primarily, the Successful Service Training Program facility will be used for Educational classrooms from the starting age of 4 to 80 years of age.

Education course is from Elementary to High school K-12 Curriculum levels. Individuals from the age of 14 years and up will move into Career school training. This portion of the education and career training programs provides enrichment courses that focus on permanently uplifting and, changing the way we think of ourselves and how we treat others around us. This goes for the Teachers, Mentors, Therapist, Counselors that are employed at our facilities. They too must be thoroughly taught before they can Uplift and teach. There must be a level of compassion, humility, and respect towards all students' members, staff and employees. Inner — city children, youths and adults will embrace our new method of education. And in the proper order of teaching for the purpose of creating confidence, happiness, and Contentment within each student member.

Problem # 2: Homelessness, Lack of
Education, Business Training Careers.

Solution #2: Successful Service Housing & Educational Arenas.

S.S.H.E.A.! This All-in-one housing, educational, career training building is magnificent! It's a 4 to 6 -story building is like a Sports Stadium Dome

Arena; public seating is 20 to 45- thousand people. The S.S.H.E.A building comes in two different services and sizes. The large ones are called "S.S.H.E.A-7 it's an advanced facility for the Public's use and its home to our graduates known as (S.S.S.H) Successful Service Superhero's"

The smaller Private S.S.H.E.A. facilities are for Student Members from the Successful Service Educational Training Programs. They must graduate in order to live in the higher advanced facility of S.S.H.E.A.-7.

What's so incredibly amazing about the structure of S.S.H.E.A.-7, it holds over 3,000 apartments and school dormitory units! Located on the top 5th and 6th floor VIP section area of the Arena Dome. Includes soundproof 1 to 4 bedrooms' apartment styled units, with overview balconies of the stadium floor. **The 4th-floor** areas are School Classrooms, cafeteria, teacher lounge and Recreational Training areas for the graduate staff members of (S.S.S.H. Successful Service Superhero's.) there's also, Board Rooms, Offices, Conference rooms for the Company's Business Administration Team, Investors and Professionals, etc. The public will not have access to these top floor levels.

The 3rd, 2nd, and 1st floor are for the Public of all ages, races, colors, and creeds. It provides the Public with Movie Theater, Public library, Computer areas, Children and Teens Gaming area. **The 2nd floor** has a Vintage Clothing and Costume Store for all ages, 7 various Restaurants, Children and Teen Toy and novelty stores, Arts & Hobby stores, Electronic, Sporting Goods store, all age Music/ Talent Video Production, etc. **The 1st floor** is the professional sport and Entertainment Stadium Arena. Hosting a variety of sporting events, Concerts, Theater play, special guest performances, Community Talent shows, Professional Modeling, etc. The outdoor left wing of the Arena is an amusement park with water slides and much more.

Each S.S.H.E.A.-7 is designed to bring a tremendous economic boost in each County, State that we serve. This extraordinary housing and entertainment service expect to bring a 90% participation success rate, by providing a wide range of celebration events such as: Hosting Bi-weekly-monthly professional NBA, NFL sporting events, Concerts performances to showcase their skills and talents for charity purposes! Ticket Pricing Sales for Public events may vary.

Private S.S.H.E.A.- Target Populations and Functionality

Problem # 3: Homelessness, Lack of Education, Business Training Careers.

Solution #3: Successful Service Housing & Educational Arenas.

Private S.S.H.E.A. Facility-1 is not a public business facility.

Dedicated to men who are recovering from Alcohol-Drug Addiction.

We accept Individuals who are recently released from Jail/Prison. Overcrowding in recent Years conditions has become quite problematic. To the point, where officials are electing to release non – violent offenders back into society. Often, these early releases backfire, since recently released inmates have nowhere to turn. So, they often wind up back behind bars to avoid a life on the streets. (S.S.H.E.A. facility -One) will provide the necessary housing, therapy, counseling, detox and education for these individuals to rebuild their lives. Once admitted, each residential Student of 16 years old and up will receive education courses, on the job training.

After a period of six months. At this time, individuals can determine if they wish to remain in the program, abandon the program, or become full – time residential Students in moving towards higher advanced Service facilities. Such as; S.S.H.E.A. -7. Additionally, each apartment will be available in 1 to 2-bedroom units with kitchen, living room, balconies and assigned bleacher seats to the entertainment Arena floor. After or during the 24 months, everyone will be expected to sustainability reaching their highest achievements imaginable.

Private S.S.H.E.A. Facility-2

Dedicated to Homeless Women/struggling Single Mothers of all ages.

Adults are not the only homeless individuals languishing along. Sadly enough, Parents with their children are forced to live amongst poverty, drug abuse, and the mentally ill. (S.S.H.E.A.-2) will provide "Safe Haven apartment units" for Women with or without Children. Ladies will have access to all the same privileges and amenities offered. Each family unit will be given up to 24 months to rebuild their lives to sustainable levels. Each apartment will be available in 1 to 5 -bedroom units with kitchen, dining room, living room, 2 bathrooms, balconies and assigned bleacher seats to the entertainment Arena floor. Additionally, some units will come fully furnished, utility free, and rent-free or based on income. The mother and child will have the opportunity to the participant within the (S.S.E.T.P) Successful Service Educational Training Programs in moving forward and reaching their highest achievements imaginable.

Private S.S.H.E.A. Facility-3.

Dedicated to Infancy to Teenage Care.

Most of these children will be referred over from various government agencies: CPS, Foster Care, Courts, Probation and Juvenile facilities. Our children's (S.S.H.E.A.- 3) would be much like the famous Harry Porter Wizardry boarding school. Holds 5 children to a room according to age. With, a large cafeteria, small school classrooms, recreational play areas and has all the comforts of home. Children to teens will enjoy the many educational school choice activities of over 35 exciting career opportunities. There is no limit on how many courses a child could pick for themselves. They could explore throughout a lifetime of learning and exploration. The adult staff members and teachers assigned to care for small Children and Teens are the student members of (S.S.S.H) The Successful Service Superheroes. Every adult member must and will treat all children as if they have given birth to them. Therefore, respectable loving care, compassion, and understanding must and will be ministered to the children and teens with no exceptions.

Private S.S.H.E.A. Facility- 4.

Dedicated towards Gang Youth Suppression, Eliminating Incarceration:

Most of these Teens to Adults will be referred over from various government agencies: State, CPS, Police Referrals, Supreme Court, Probation, Felony. We will Youth Starting from across America, Los Angeles, Riverside, Oakland and, San Bernardino County will be utilizing the many services provided by The Successful Service Training Programs. It is understood that many of these youths will have certain gang affiliations. To that end, all youth with gang affiliations who reached our S.S.H.E.A. facility. Due to having excellent behavioral skills, respect for themselves and for others around them. If an individual does not possess any of these attributes, then they will remain in the Community Evaluation Processing facility. Until they can live up to the standards of S.S.H.E.A. Individuals will be properly placed into certain S.S.H.E.A. Facilities according to their zips coded area. This ensures that each youth can maneuver safely and freely throughout their Housing Facility. Our goal is to give an individual the necessary education, skills, and knowledge to uphold themselves as a prominent citizen of social society. To ultimately demonstrate positivity to those who were once arched enemies willing to work together as (SSSH) Successful Service Superheroes!

Katherine's Magical Revitalization Economic Community Development Services Inc.

Executive Summary

Introduction

Katherine's Magical Revitalization Economic Community Development Initiative. Provides financial information; it includes the basic strategic information necessary for initial establishment and operation for the State of California. Outlining plans for Nationwide- Worldwide Economic Empowerment Growth on a Grand Scale Level. And provides the tactics for Unlimited Community Participation through the <u>Successful Service Educational Training Programs.</u> The Business Plan provides Business profit potentials, methods, procedures for operation infrastructure, management for the development and expansion. Put together as the world's most profitable Business Conglomerate Enterprises. Expected to generate first annual sales profit of $1-Trillion U.S. American Dollars.

Katherine's Magical Revitalization Community Development; works as a Self-Governing, Economic Community development Service throughout the Urban Inner-City and Rural Impoverished areas in America. The Company comes with its own <u>Katherine's Magical Indigenous Constitutional Law Decree</u>. It's the instructional base Policy of our Rules and Regulations that must be admitted, abide and highly respected as it is written by the Indigenous Law.

Our Economic Community Development Plan consists of (7 out of 13) Enterprise Business Conglomerates" for unlimited national/worldwide Potential sales profit. Allowing each residential community to financially sustain itself through its own community business service. Through partnerships with the <u>Successful Service Social Programs Inc.</u> Our nationwide social service provides Millions of New Jobs, Career/ Business Training opportunities for eager Americans. To participate in the transformation development and management of Katherine's Magical Revitalization Residential and Business Service. This would give our society a much-needed lift for all Inner-City, Rural Impoverished areas a much Safer, Sustainable, Prosperous Economic Future.

Each K.M.R.C.D. Community must have a solid financial structural basis for continuous economic growth and empowerment for the State. Each business service would be Securely situated around all K.M.R.C.D. Residential Community areas; for enjoyment, safety, comfort, and convenience. Community support and participation of our business services are assured! Our Economic Community Development Plan consists of over (7) Enterprise Conglomerates" of unlimited national/worldwide sales profit potential. Allowing each residential community to financially sustain itself through its own generated business and community development service. Partnering with the Successful Service Training Programs of S.S.H.E.A. Would give our society the ultimate Transformation famously known as;

"The Promise Land -Meets- Theme Park Heaven"
One K.M.R.E.C.D.S. includes but is not limited to:

- Katherine's Magical Residential Housing Community.
- Successful Service Housing and Educational Arena's (S.S.H.E. A'S)
- Financial Gold Protection Law Banking Branch.
- The Place of Dreams" World's Largest Theme Park.
- Katherine's Magical Ancient Museum.
- Katherine's Magical Mega Warehouse Store.
- Katherine's Magical Get Away Retreat Resorts.
- K. M Paradise Cruise Ship Travel, Airline, Transportation Services. The Following is the Company Business Initiatives.

Problem #4 Lack of Exploration, Entertainment, and Enlightenment

Solution #4 The Place of Dreams Theme Parks

The Place of Dreams will stand as the centerpiece of our entertainment public services. All services mentioned are in close proximity of each other and are all located at all front Public establishment's areas of K.M.R.C. Private Residential Community areas. K.M.R.C. is the highest level that is privately secured. All Theme Parks will be located outside of all Urban City areas because there is not enough land development to place 9 to 13 thousand acres in the middle of Urban areas. We suggest nearby Rural Areas. Moreover, the story of Katherine Irvin and the Place of Dreams Theme Park" will be chronicled in the Arrival of the Promise Land" film project.

We firmly believe that the Place of Dreams will be the largest Theme Park in America and will make all other theme parks (Disneyland, Knott's Berry Farm, and Magic Mountain) obsolete. The Place of Dreams will be label by the general public as the most extraordinary theme park in the world. It's time for you and your family to experience a new kind of theme park. One of the reasons why this theme park is so large and so unique is because of the unique main attractions and housing community that surrounds it. The Place of Dreams will forever change not only the way you view Theme Parks but the way everyone views their own neighborhood community! We feel that the primary reason individuals visit a theme park is to unwind from a stressful week. While some individuals may go for a family vacation, or to give the children a wonderful time of adventure and exploration, at the Place of Dreams, we want it to be a memorable experience.

The Place of Dreams theme park will instantly capture your attention by what it doesn't have. No roller coasters; No lame Prize booths with the same lame prizes. Instead, The Place of Dreams has a variety of unique Fantasy Land Adventure Neighborhoods! Each with their own unique style of character, exploration and adventure appeal. These adventure Neighborhoods cater to any person wildest dreams imagined and are sure to have something for every member of the family. Here is a sampling of some of the awesome main attractions that await you.

- Neighborhood Time Travel Adventures Dreams
- Kandy Land Kingdom Dreams & Restaurant and Sweet Shops
- Whimsical Fantasy Land Dreams
- Universe Galaxy Dreams
- Super Summer Fun Land Dreams
- The Scariest Haunted Neighborhood (Your Nightmare Dreams)
- Video Game Action Neighborhood Dreams
- Unique Classic Drive-In Theater Dreams
- Restaurants that cater to adults and children alike.
- Your Musical Neighborhood Dreams
- Weird and Wacky Dreams
- Adventure Exploration Dreams
- And much, much more!

The Place of Dreams was created in hopes of providing a much- needed escape in these turbulent times. Even, if only for a few hours, this escape will truly change your life. With most theme parks, the fun ends at closing time. Not at the Place of Dreams. We offer a variety of overnight packages such as 3-Day to a Weekly vacation plan are available. Even better, it's designed for tourist and national customers to stay in the Dream Land Neighborhood of their choice! You will come to find a truly extraordinary experience. The Place of Dreams was created with the concept of stretching your imagination beyond its limits.

Theme Park Specialized Transportation.

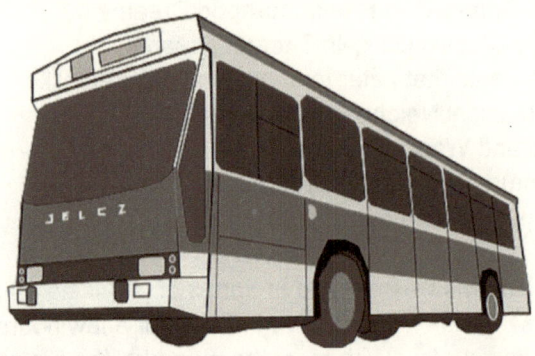

Pricing will vary, 24- hour Online ticket sales or at location tickets booths will operate from 8:00 am to closing, daily. *Special* discount rates will apply to all Successful Service Employee members, Students, and Staff.

Transportation issues will also be a thing of the past. Katherine's Magical Revitalization Economic services will sponsor buses that will pick – up individuals at the designated pick – up points throughout our service area. The buses will provide non – stop transportation to and from the theme parks areas, up until two hours after the park's closing. This bus service will be provided to the public at no charge! Talk about a transit plan!

Katherine's Magical Ancient Museum

Our Ancient artifacts and materials from the past will speak volumes to those who have returned. All Ancient Artifacts will be promptly displayed for all to see what life was like some millions of years prior. All stolen Ancient Ancestry Artifacts, materials, clothing items, and writings will come from various European museums like the Smithsonian, British, France, top floor and basement levels and private homes. These items that are currently stolen must be returned to the rightful Descendants of the Indigenous Negro Population and place carefully into our Magical Ancient Museum. Our Museum will be located wherever the Place of Dreams Theme Parks are at. This unique service gives the long-awaited its final resting place. Members will receive a historical connection, education, and inside information and great knowledge. More details of this Extraordinary Museum will be forth coming.

Problem #5 Lack of Exploration, Adventurous Entertainment & Excitement.

Solution #5 Katherine's Magical Paradise Travel Packages

The Company is planning on obtaining 7 luxury Cruise ships for 24 hours pick up and arrivals to either destination sides of the country. This is an exclusive international travel program that will allow student members (Who have passed a certain level of the Successful Service Training program- S.S.H.E.A.) To live, work, play and explore. Students will have the opportunity to create various career opportunities on coastal areas of Africa's Ivory Coast, Cairo Egypt, Ethiopia, the Land of Kush, Jamaica, Thailand, Cambodia, Isle Grenada, Caribbean Islands, Haiti, South America, Cuba and more. The major concept behind this project service is to expand the minds of the Indigenous Negro American Student members.

For far too long, too many Urban residents have not seen the light beyond urban strife. This travel package program will give Students members the opportunity to work towards the development of other S.S.H.E.A. Facilities throughout the Continents that are mentioned. For Tourist only; once operations are fully completed within various cities lands mentioned. Only then will our public tourist attraction services be available to the general public. Using participating Prepaid Card provided by (F.G.P.L.C Banking Branch.

Problem #6: Poverty, Lack of Emergency Financial Assistance, High Cost of Living, Lack of Legal Representation, Hostile Government forces, Uncivilized Citizens, Unwarranted Automotive Policy, IRS Tax, Unfair Passports policy.

Solution #6: Financial Gold Protection Law Card and Banking Branch.

I, Katherine Irvin, Founder, President, and CEO Hereby, introduces the "Financial Gold Protection Law Card, Banking Branch Institution." The F.G.P.L.C. Banking Branch is to ensure investment funding spending is being properly utilized for inner-city safety, economic growth, residential support and participation for nationwide sustainability. Consider the way many company's finances are being managed can be the difference between success and failure. We are managing our finances through the Company's Banking Institution. Failure of this service would be virtually impossible!

We plan to obtain various Companies within the U.S. necessary for initial operation and establishment. Our technical Banking service collects and stores all sales transaction data, from all Business service that our company provides.

We compile the data of consumerism, sales revenue of our business services. Then it is automatically divided into capital payouts to the interests of the Student Members, investors, funders, employees, hired corporations, administrative staff, etc. Capitol payouts are distributed by annually, Monthly or Weekly depending on the interested party member and Student member. We also provide services such as Checking, Savings, Bill Pay and Loans.

The unique aspect about our banking service is it provides Emergency Financial assistance, Free Legal Assistance, Protection and Safety Service for student members of the program. We intend to provide Student members with School/College supplies, stylish Uniforms with member Merit Badges. For the prevention from any unwanted hostel citizen, police harassment, stalking and abuse. By using their personalized (F.G.P.L.C.) Financial Gold Protection Law Card. To ensure the safety and wellbeing of the student member traveling from wherever our Company services are at.

Example F.G.P.L.C Front and Backside.

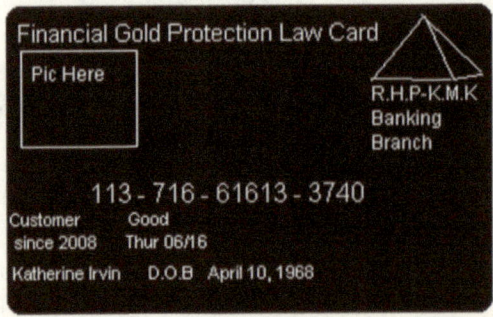

F.G.P.L. Prepaid Membership Card Service, for all Ages, Races and Nationality._S.S.H.E.A. entertainment service would be one of our most profitable business services in America. Local and International tourist will participant in the purchase of their one- Prepaid Membership card. To shop at any one of our Theme Park Service. The card is used in the same way, Costco and other whole stores are used. Customers will deposit any amount of money into their F.G.P.L. Per-Paid Membership Card. This will allow customers to access any one of Katherine's Magical Revitalization Business services throughout America and the World! Customers will save big on all popular merchandise, products, and services that are sold at any one of Katherine's Magical Super Mega Stores. Moreover, the public at large will have the opportunity to deposit money on their card to purchase any one of our amazing services and are not limited to the following:

- Katherine's Magical Revitalization Business Services.
- Public Business Services of the S.S.H.E.A.
- Amusement /Theme Park Services
- Legal Protection Services
- Transportation Services

F.G.P.L.C. Financial Gold Protection Law Prepaid Card Service

Customers from all over the world, including customers who do not necessarily qualify for our Public Social Service Programs. Can still enjoy themselves at any one of our amazing Theme Park, entertainment and business service outlets! By simply purchasing a one-time $50.00-dollar fee for their F.G.P.L Prepaid Card. To deposit any amount of money onto their Prepaid Card which will allow them to gain access at any one of K.M.R.E.C.D. Business Service outlets and save big on all Popular Brand- Name Products, Foods, Merchandise, Latest Electronics, Clothing, Furniture you name it! Any item being sold at any one of Katherine's Magical Mega Super Store. K.M.R.E.C.D.S Business Services includes but are not limited to the following:

1. Place of Dreams Theme Park, Hotel Retreats
2. S.S.H.E.A. Successful Service Housing & Educational Arena's #7
3. S.S.H.E.A. Magical Mega Super Store
4. Katherine's Magical Ancient Museum
5. Katherine's Sanctuary Nature Gardens
6. Paradise Cruise Ship & Airport Travel service
7. Katherine's Magical Paradise Travel service.

Problem #7: Police Brutality, Crimes, Government Tyranny, Lack of Safety Patrol, Lack of Positive Role Models.

Solution #7 (F.G.P.L.C) Protection and Safety Service

This service can only be accessible by using your Personalized Financial Gold Protection Law Card. All participating students and employee's cardholders of the F.G.P.L.C Bank will be provided with mini surveillance cameras that can be attached to their vehicles or clothing. These cameras will come in handy during any encounter with law enforcement or citizen altercations, kidnapping, rape attempts and attacks. Now, any police misconduct can be directly reported to the Financial Gold Protection Law Bank Legal Department or the offending agency.

With just the push of a button will immediately alert the "Safety Protection Leaders" to the aid of the cardholder. Our Safety Protection Leaders are highly trained professionals from the Successful Service Training Programs. Their properly trained to conduct policing actions necessary to maintain peace and equal fairness on both side of the spectrum. If according to the recorded evidence, the officer is indeed guilty of any misconduct, the officer will be required to pay a fine ranging from $500.00 to $500,000.00 within thirty to 60 days. This fine will be in addition to any other restitution payments deemed necessary by a court of law located inside the {SSSP} Television Station Network & Hall of Justice Court House} will be placed automatically on the "The Financial Gold Protection Law Card."

Problem #8: United States Government Corruption, Illegal U.S. Bombardments & Invasive Intrusions, Police Stalking, Brutality, Senseless Murders, Violent Hostile Citizens.

Solution #8: Protection Leaders- SSSH Successful Service Superheroes!

This service can only be accessed using the Financial Gold Protection Law Card- Member Service. Our Safety Protection Leaders are the graduates of Successful Service Educational Arenas. Who have become the Successful Service Superheroes! These Men and Women are from the starting age of 18 teen years the overall "Mind Set and Everyday Intentions" of our Protection Safety Leaders of (SSSH) is composed of Integrity, Intelligence, Great Compassion, Respect, Common Sense, and Kindness. Therefore, what better candidates to protect and serve our Streets and Neighborhoods from all up evils other than our Safety Protection Leaders of course!

Highly skilled trained Graduates from the Successful Service Training Program Facility of S.S.H.E.A. are well-trained individuals that work to Serve and Protect ANYONE no matter what Race or Nationality. Our Sovereign Law Decreed is appointed and Secured by way of Indigenous Human Rights. It is their Authoritative Right to ensure Safety and Protection within and around S.S.H.E.A and K.M.R.E.C.D. Communities Land, Air, and Sea.

This protection agency applies to if the situation warrants itself necessary to do so. All members of (SSSH) have the same if not more Authoritative right as any U.S. Government Official, Presidents, Military, Police officer, Sheriff, Lawyer, Court Judge, etc. Based upon Common Sense and logical reasoning of their Survival and Human Rights. And based upon themselves Being Indigenous to their own Country"

Our Safety Protection Leaders will be assigned with Legal Mentors and Guardians of intelligence to stand as witnesses and to encourage all participants to be on their best behavior in and outside of our service areas. The instructions applied by Law through The Company's Law Decree attachment.

All requested Safety and Protection service will be Monitored and Recorded live in real time through F.G.P.L. Banking Branch Institution, Monitoring, and Surveillance Network System. For immediate analyzes and reviewing of all encounters and situations. To prevent any confrontation from happening, Cardholders will be provided with Unique Uniforms, Company Constitutional Law Badges and mini surveillance cameras that can be attached to their vehicles or clothing.

<u>The Law Decree Badges and Surveillance Cameras</u> lets everyone know who the Individual affiliations are. It prevents them from any Police Encounters, Questioning, Brutality, U.S. Government Corruption, and uncivilized hostile Citizens. We will inform all U.S. Government Officials, Police Officer, Court Judges, Senators, Presidents, Military, Lawyers, of the rules and regulations. Through various public meetings in Congress, Court Meeting, News Announcement, Radio, Social Media, and conferences to ensure our Indigenous Human Rights will NOT be tampered with nor violated.

Any U.S. Police, Military, Attorney, Judge or Priest commits ANY misconduct or violations will be immediately reported to the Successful Service Legal Department or the offending agency. And with just the push of a button will immediately alert and send out the (Safety Protection Leaders of S.S.S.H) to the aid of the Participant, Residents, Employee Staff Members, and Tourist Customers. Our Safety Team is properly trained to conduct <u>Policing Enforcement Actions</u> necessary to maintain safety and equal fairness. If our Safety Protectors- S.S.S.H is forced to Protect the victims and themselves then it shall be done "<u>By ANY Means Necessary</u>" It's extremely important to read request our Companies Historical Identity report and Constitutional Law Decree. To get a better understanding of why it's crucially important for our services to be developed

Problem #9: Lack of State Citizen Support & Participation. False Television Media Reporting. United States Government Corruption, Illegal U.S. Bombardments & Invasive Intrusions, Police Stalking, Brutality, Senseless Murders, Violent Hostile Citizens.

Solution #9: The People's Public Media Courthouse. (By way of Indigenous Human Rights Law)

This service can be only accessible using the F.G.P.L. Card Member Service. The People's Hall of Justice Public Media Courthouse, work side by side as the People's Public Legal Team. The Public of any age, race or creed will be given access to their platform. To Publicly address their immediate need within our Public Media Court House. We don't just expose and report issues relating to only Black Indigenous Americans issues. We also cover various sectors in all situations good and bad of extremely important issues that are affecting us all today. We will look to have the guilty removed from their positions if the incident in question is egregious enough to warrant such consideration.

As mentioned, the Successful Service Social Program is arduously working to help gain the freedom of individuals who have been falsely/wrongly imprisoned under the U.S. Government. Each day the People's Hall of

Justice Media Court will chronicle the story of people of Police Brutality and false imprisonment throughout America. Upon close examination and investigation of case files, the People's Legal Team will aid individuals with the most legitimate claims of wrongful/false imprisonment. Too often, justice in this country has only worked for the people Who are controlling the "System" to their advantage. Finally, there is legal representation for the long-suffering people of the inner – city that truly needs to have the law on their side.

F.G.P.L.C. Gold Mining Service

This service can only be accessible by using your Personalized Financial Gold Protection Law Card. Our financial foundation for the entire company of K.M.R.E.C.D.S is in the form of "Gold and U.S Dollar Currency funding" This service Provides financial Gold payouts towards Student members, Employees, Hired companies and professionals alike. Our Mining company which provides gold, gems, and precious metals to individuals who are interested in receiving gold payments payouts in the form of gold coins the size of half dollars, gold tablets and gold bricks. This would be placed inside their safe deposit box located at our banking branch or kept wherever is most comfortable for that individual or company.

Participants also have the option of melting a small portion of their gold piece into any creative shape, tool or jewelry that they wish. For participants, the amount of gold you have is the amount of money you have on your F.G.P.L. Card. Monthly or Yearly gold payouts amounts will depend on the person participation, efforts, and achievements. The gold payments can be converted into U.S. American Dollars. This service also provides residents with the ability to purchase groceries, clothing, and pay utility bills, etc.

There is no need to fret; the F.G.P.L. Card will be accepted anywhere credit, and debit cards are accepted.

Problem #10 Illegal Public or Private Zoo's, Pet Stores, Circuses etc.

Solution#10: Katherine's Magical Wild- life Sanctuary & Getaway Retreats

This wildlife Sanctuary is perfect for Animals who were captured and placed in illegal public Zoo's, Pet Store, Animal Storage, Circus, Carnivals, events, etc. We investigate and educate the U.S. Government on Animal Cruelty. The Indigenous Law Decree prohibits any use of government services for control, possession and entertainment purposes. Animals have the same Indigenous Rights as all others and should be protected from any unwarranted government interferences.

This Wildlife Sanctuary is confirmed into many different Animal lifestyle sections for the comfort and safety of the inhabitants. While placed at our Sanctuary the Animal will eventually be relocated at their original natural location from around the world of the Promise land natural areas.

Katherine's Magical Nature Garden Retreats

Katherine's Magical Nature Garden Retreats is perfect for those who just want to get away from it all. This service is located throughout America's Rural areas and serves as an Area of Recreational Wildlife Forestry Resorts. It has Hiking Trails and Exploration, Camping Areas, Fruit & Vegetable Picking, Gold Mining Adventures and Cave Explorations. The entire landmass contains a variety of lush Fruit, Vegetables, Nuts and Spice Garden, Exotic Trees, Flowers, and Plants, along with other botanical treats to please as far as the eyes can see. Customers will have the opportunity to plan a community meeting center where customers can plan group activities or just simply unwind after a long day of exploration. The Gardens will serve as host to various events throughout the year including school tours and camping trips. Family or single retreat.

The Gardens will be maintained exclusively by S.S.S.H. These Wildlife Retreats are high, secured and will be monitored 24-hours a day, and 7 days a week. This security coverage will consist of a joint effort between the S.S.S.H. and its Surveillance cameras that forwards the Animal rescue or Human Rescue activity immediately back to the secured booths and headquarters to the patrol areas.

Family Fun Nature Workshops

Whether you garden for beauty and for food production, these season-appropriate various garden workshops will guide our citizens through the steps of getting a garden started and maintaining it in an organic and sustainable manner. Learn the basics of gardening without harmful pesticides or chemical fertilizers that pollute our surrounding land and waterways. We teach you how to garden property and eat Healthily.

Energy Efficient Wildlife Retreat Homes!

Example Photo from;

We also provide unique energy efficient pyramid style homes that are constructed into beautiful and very spacious 1 to 8-bedroom, four-story home with wrap around balcony porch. These unique homes compliment the wildlife wilderness areas. And are only located in the Highly Advanced Promise Land.

For electricity usage would apply solar panels and natural heating conductors for individual homes. Ordinary Roof Surfaces often provides the largest percentages of impervious surface on a site. The impact on the surrounding environment is that stormwater is not absorbed where it lands. By holding stormwater where it falls. It can evaporate naturally into the environment and the groundwater table at a slow and steady rate. One way to accomplish this is by "Greening the Roof, in which the Roof connects to the ground. By building each home half-way below the ground surface and adding grass and plants to the roof surface. This approach acknowledges the principle that the natural ways of cleaning air and water are the best ways of living.

Katherine's Magical Television Station Network.

The Katherine's Magical Worldwide Television Network/ Internet service will air it's the Company Services 6 months prior to the grand opening of the Featured Movie/Firm is released. Provide viewers with the opportunity to vote or celebrate on the matters that affect their communities and way of life the most. Television Station Network/Internet service is one of our biggest promotion and marketing tool we have. This marketing strategy will allow both companies to concentrate their resources on the greatest opportunities. To increase sales and achieve sustainable competitive advantage. Our promotional, marketing service will air all services mentioned three months prior to the Grand opening of the Place of Dreams Theme, S.S.H.E.A #7, Trips to Paradise Travels, Katherine's Magical Ancient Museum, Neighborhood Processing Facility, Katherine's magical warehouse store, Secured Nature Gardens and Financial Gold Protection Law Card-Banking Branch.

The Conclusion of our truly Amazing Services is just a small portion that was just outlined. The end results of our Development would easily Change America and the World into a Real- Life Promise Land of your own making.

Because most of us currently live in a "<u>Hellish Existence</u>". Therefore, the Balance of "<u>Good</u>" must emerge from within it.

Katherine's Syfy Film Trilogy Bonus!

Character Description:
KATHERINE Single Mother of four, Unaware that something extraordinarily amazing beyond her imagination is coming her way.

[ACTION]
"Katherine" a mother of four, is encapsulated by poverty, living in a homeless shelter due to the high cost of living. She sees her friends and family members involved in Illegal mass incarceration, police brutality, gang violence. That leads to devastating situations caused by government corruption. She sees her closest friends being brutally attacked by Police. The Police then attempts to turn the attack on Katherine, she runs away and escapes from her would be Police attacker and hides behind a building and rests. Thinking of her children she quickly heads back to the homeless shelter; she finds them safe playing with other children. She then looks out the window to see the Police running pass the window. Just then she is being yelled at by the homeless director of being late for the daily mandatory meetings. And, is threatening that she will be kicked out if she's late again. Comforted by her children Katherine believes there's no hope to her situation. She retreats to her room and starts to continue to do her work on her computer she's determined to finish her Project Development Plan. A plan so great it will ultimately change the world into the Promise Land.

As her children sleep She types into the night, that morning she sends her children off to school, as she stands at the corner waving goodbye to her children she hears foot's steps walking up behind her, she turns around and it's the same corrupt Police that was chasing her before. They arrest her because Katherine saw something, they did not want her to see. The police take Katherine down to the station to threaten and intimidate her not to testify in court of what she saw.

They threaten that she will never see her Children again if she told what happens. So, she agreed, and they let her go. Her friend who was attacked by the police is counting on Katherine's support to testify against the Police. And is unaware that the Police had threatened Katherine. Katherine ends up testifying against the Police anyway. The Police illegally take Katherine to jail for nothing. She has No money for an attorney she waits for a court-appointed an attorney. That works together with the Police and the prosecuting attorney. Katherine sits in her cell alone, worried for her children she starts to cry. Suddenly a light appears in the top right corner of her cell, the light becomes brighter and brighter that she puts her hands in front of her face to block out the light.

Katherine barely could see, squinting her eyes and sees a figure, a person standing in one corner and another person standing at another corner. She completely opens her eyes there are three women in her room extremely tall stood about 15 Feet high. Katherine cannot understand why she isn't frightened by what she is seeing. These Dimensional Beings are Beautiful, and their clothing is unusually neat and perfect. Katherine cannot understand how her jail cell suddenly became very large. Looking around noticing that the room has a high ceiling when it wasn't high before, noticing that the tall beings' shoes are very shiny and are not touching the ground. Just then she hears a voice in her head of a man saying Hello ------ a name that she cannot say because it is of her Spiritual name from eons ago. That name that was called to Katherine made her break down and cry because she suddenly remembers who she is.

Katherine is shown in her mind's eye that she is a God like Being" from another Primal World, with unimaginable powers. She sees herself operating one of the largest Ship in the Galaxy. To a human -eyes the "Ship" has the look and size of a Planet. But it is neither a Planet nor a Ship, It is something she cannot describe. She has shown through her mind's eyes the Land she once lived on. And, that land is of the most Beautiful Place beyond a human's comprehension.

The Galactic Being of a Women's voice; "You will create this land of Beauty and wonderment and Magic in the Land that is most Troubled of where you live now. In the troubled land of where we placed you at long ago"

Katherine; why did you place me here? Why would you leave me down here on earth when you know it is hell on earth, why?"

Galactic Beings; we placed all of our children here, we placed them in many different lands throughout the world." [As the beings are talking, Katherine is shown a vision in time of large motherships landing dropping people off in various Countries and States from around the world] Katherine recognizes her family, relatives, friends and millions of other black people being placed in America, South America, Mexico, Asia, Europe you named it".

Beings voice: "We will place you in unfortunate situations that will trigger the greatest solution idea of that problem that you are in.

Katherine then begins to write the greatest solution to Homelessness. She is stunned by what she came up with. At that moment she sees in her mind's eye the vision of the "Women Being" fading out of sight as if she implanted the idea in her mind. Katherine completes the housing solution and is shocked by the details of the plan. Katherine later finds an apartment is now with her children. The writer professionally types it just the way she instructs it should be. For the next 10 years, Katherine suffers under most of the worst impoverished conditions and has witnessed more government abuse then she liked to admit. The date is September 2011 America is covered in Tyranny and Poverty, the FBI, CIA and Police department is relentless in their deception and corrupt acts against the people for their support in mass incarceration, government-hired gang violence, and Police stalking, and harassment is at an all-time high.

Horrible situations that are caused by the U.S government, whether it be the victimization of her family and friends or if it's directly happening to Katherine. She now has the ability to write the Ultimate Solution plan designed to save millions of people from poverty, crimes, murder, and corruption. And, replacing it with the most Amazing Project Development plans that America has ever seen! She forms it all together creating the Authored Book that your reading right now. Incredible Project Development Plans that's designed to create the Promise Land, and a New Alternative Reparation BILL ACT for Congress Assembled, the State Senate and the U.S. Supreme Court to review and bring forth the Approval for a long-awaited overdue Legislation Bill!

Finally, she sends her work to the United States Congress and the President of the United States. Un-note to Katherine or any other citizen the U.S. Military, Congress and the President is visited by the "Otherworldly Begins", They are informed by a sudden presence in the atmosphere that stopped all central intelligence communications, scanners, radars on land and sea. All airways and transmitters are completely nonfunctional. Every single employee, news media, the Pentagon, Congress, all employees at Capitol Hill are confused. The space satellite is being physically compromised by a large UFO presence shutting down its functions as it passes through their atmosphere. It's the most incredible sight to see and the most horrible sight to see for others indeed!

The UFO appears entering over Washington D.C. Whitehouse and Capitol Hill and it's becoming clear to everyone in government only. Six of the Beings come down from their Ship floating through the top roof and into the Oval Office. Where the President sits stiffly in the middle of a press conference. About an upcoming Nuclear War that is scheduled to take place within the week between the U.S. Iran, Cuba, Russia and more. Everyone is completely still, nothing is moving. These Galactic Beings are different quite disturbing and Creepy Actually. They calmly speak to everyone in and outside of the White House telepathically.

[Description: 15ft tall Bug Insect]

Galactic Mantis Speaks: I am speaking only to my European children. (Government) For many, many years you have brought much pain and anguish to the Indigenous god-like people of earth. You know you don't belong in this world. You come from another world that was destroyed by our own kind. But we saved you, we saved what was left of you and we placed you here on earth in hopes that you'd be a wonderful asset to the god-like people of Earth. But as we can see your efforts for any hope have all been Fruitless and Vile. You all turned out to be gods of Evil causing destruction and tyranny throughout the lands that are not of your own. But of course, all things including evil must come to an end. And, so we are here to collect our European Children."

Suddenly, screams are heard throughout Capitol Hill in the streets, in houses, apartment windows, businesses, cars, parks and everywhere. The ones who are screaming are being ripped and torn by a dark shadowy entity. Bystanders stare in horror as they witness Certain Selected People screaming and being physically tormented then quickly snatched up and taken into another dimension into the abyss of darkness.

Galactic Mantis Speaks; The ones who are not collected must do a great service to the Indigenous god-like people of Earth. And you must allow the New Project called "The New Alternative Reparation Plan" to form without any interruption in its progress of development or thereafter. If there is any interruption in its progress of development? Then someone within your closes circle will be terminated, one by one in various horrific ways. We are fully aware, there is a war brewing within your own government between the Democrats and the Republicans. In fact, we will make sure that the fighting intensifies because a greater and lesser "Evil" is within the two parties. That refuses to compromise with one another based on your personal feelings and hatred towards each other. The question is which of the two evils will stop the progress of the Reparation Plan from moving forward? Will it be the Democrats who were in support of Slavery because they despise the Indigenous god-like population but only pretended to be on their side only when Election days came around. After the Election is over, they continue to unleash tyranny onto the innocent people. And how about those Republicans who stood by for so long and watch the entire Country fall apart by Slavery, Racial injustices, and Oppression. Your deliberate Bias Complacency has caused an equal amount of destruction and tyranny against the Indigenous of Earth.

Both sides had the power the resources and support of the people to create Heaven on earth. But instead, both sides would rather create Hell on earth because that's where most of you were created from. That's right, you were conceived by entities that were avoided of souls. And which that place you were created you must return. The process will begin for the annihilation of your "Containers" (The Body) and none of you will have control over what will be done to you. Everything that you placed upon the Indigenous god-like people of the earth will come back to you 7 times greater"

THE MEDIA NEWS; reports hit the airways on the vicious attacks and murder of "Certain people" throughout American and the World, people who are connected with the U.S. Government. Whether by Bloodline, Employment or Closes Association. The entire situation was orchestrated by the Galactic Mantis Beings 400 hundred years ago. It is with gladness and excitement of the notion to finally use the government's deadly downfall as "Harvest Time" Feeding off the pain of their energy is how the Galactic Mantis Beings" Survives". The white news broadcaster starts to cry Live on Air. He tries to pull himself together but sits in utter horror as he tries to give the daily announcements. He dares not turn around because the announcement about the Galactic Mantis Beings Ripping people is now Standing directly behind him! This thing stands directly behind him and gives him a Telepathic Vision what they just did to his entire family. (Trust me you don't want to know what they did)

Suddenly Chaos and confusion erupt, the sky opens, and Billions of Spaceships are flying into our atmosphere making all kind of maneuvers, zipping and soaring through the nighttime sky with an array of the most beautiful bright colors. Some people are running scared out of their minds, while others are standing in shock and amazement. Suddenly nuclear bombs and meteorites begin to fall in the most frightening scene of all times. Crashing and crushing buildings, homes, and People. 70% of all Indigenous Negro Americans and African Americans-God like people of the earth starts to disappear in thin air. They end-up on Huge Motherships appearing in various large rooms. Some people who were picked up by the ships were crying hysterically out of control from thinking the bombs had hit them. While others look completely confused and some were utterly happy high fiving each other saying: Wow man we did it, we did it, we made it!! Two very tall Galactic Black men who were the overseers of the ship came over to the happy people and informed them that they're finally going home to their original Paradise Planet. The people cheered and cried from sheer happiness, they asked where is the planet at?

The Galactic Tall Black men; your home is directly behind the Sun.

[Suddenly the window of the ship opens and reveals the Sun] And their headed straight through it. And their all-in amazement at what the Sun really is. It's a gateway a portal to another dimension and as we passed through it, we are given something to drink that puts us all to sleep. When we awoke from our 7- hour sleep we are changed into the most Powerful people in the Universe.

The End

UFO/Alien Encounters

Description of my earliest to my most recent UFO/ALIEN Abduction Incidences.

A Brief Background

[For privacy purposes I refer to my Children names as Child 1,2,3,4]

I'm a Part-time Student majoring in Fashion Design, Urban Planning. My hobbies are working on Community Development Project to change America. I'm a mother of 4 wonderful Children. Child 1. age 29, Child 2 age 27, Child 3 age 20 and my Child 4 age 17.

My childhood was happy, boring, Magical and normal. You know, Mother, Father, 3 siblings, assorted animals, white Pickett fence the whole nine yards. I grew up in Grand Rapids Michigan for 19 Years. My mother, two siblings and I abruptly moved to Phoenix Az in February of 1986 due to my parent's divorce. And I lived in Phoenix for 13 Years. I then moved to Los Angeles California in August of 2000 with my three children at the time. Since then I moved to various locations throughout California due to the high cost of living.

1973 UFO-Alien Incidences:
I was 5- years old living in Grand Rapids Michigan when I saw a Diamond and long shaped Spacecraft floating above my next -door neighborhoods house. As it was floating away from our house, I was waving goodbye.

Another incidence around that same age, I found myself standing between two male figures, {I do not know what their faces or body look like} We seemed to be in a Space ship because we were looking out of a huge window of space in the sky watching all kinds of different colored Spaceships doing all kinds of flips, turns twist and maneuvers. One male was shorter than the other male. And the shorter one said that I had to go back home. I then started crying, so bad that my stomach started hurting. So, the Short one told me the funniest Joke I ever heard in my life. {It was a dark humor Joke from the voice of my Father} I laughed so hard that I fell on the floor. Falling through the floor still laughing, landing onto my bed. Waking my sister up from laughing.

Summer of 1979 UFO Abduction Incident of my Sister:

I was 11 years old and my Sister was 9. Living in Grand Rapids Michigan. We were suddenly happy to find out that we were going on a 2- week Summer camping trip. In which my Mother signed us up for Summer Camp. So, I ended up in one Cabin with a group of girls and my sister ended up at another Cabin because she was in the younger children's group. We're about 5-6 days in our Camp stay when suddenly a tall male Camp Counsellor. Asked if, I, my sister and about 3 other girls out of 100 or more kids. Wanted to go on a little Camp hike and cookout. We ended up cooking delicious Smores and Hot Dogs while listening to the Camp Counsellor tell a very scary story. About a woman who got her head cut off in the woods, we were staying at. In which her spirit still roams around the exact same area that we were at called "**The Sand Dunes**" telling us kids to "Never roam here at night." So, we finished our camping adventure and heading back to our cabins.

While walking, back to our cabins I kept wondering why would he take us out here just to tell us "Children" that scary story? We all went to bed at around 8:00 or 9:00 Pm. Later, that night around 3:00 am I woke up to what sounded like my sister yelling and banging on the outside of her cabin door. Saying "Let me in! Heeey! Let me in!!! Now I knew that wasn't her because I felt that would be impossible given the situation that we're in. So, I turned over and went back to sleep. That morning I was woken up by my sisters camp Counsellors asking me questions like: "Does your sister Sleepwalk? I said "No," they asked "Well has she ever Slept Walked before? I said, "No she never Slept walked in her life". Then I later went outside and saw a group of adults surrounding my Sister asking her questions. So, I waited over by the Tree until they finished. I asked my Sister what happened? and she said. "I don't know, all I know is I found myself looking up in the night sky with my arms stretched out. Looking around I found myself standing right in the middle of the "**Sand Dunes!**" Where that lady got her head chopped off at. And then I ran as fast as I could back to the Cabin".

So, I said "But there was no way you could've gotten out of the door because you need the Key to unlock the door from the inside. And only the Camp Counselors have Keys. And the windows were too narrow and high for you to reach. So, how did you get outside then? My Sister said. "I don't know, and the camp counselors don't know either". And then my Sister said "maybe a Spaceship took me. Do you believe me?" And I said,

"Of course but why did they take you and not me?" I'm older than you!" {I was feeling a little Jealous}

I believe that my Sisters abductors wanted me to know that they took her. Because they knew that I would later doubt their existence. And that this incident would be later used as "Confirmation"

Out of Body or Premonition Incident? April of 1995 Phoenix AZ, (Age 27)

I took my 2 Children, age 4 and age 6 to Mac Donald's. The children were playing in the Jungle Gym area of the Restaurant. I was sitting at the table looking outside the window. When suddenly I found myself in another place or time? It looked like a film crew of directors and film staff members surrounding me. As they were working on the production of a film? The situation I was in felt as though I was "<u>Extraordinarily Important"</u> as if I were the focus for some sort of movie event? I quickly came back into my Consciousness and said, "What the hell was that?!" Looking around at my surroundings I didn't understand what just happen or why I saw that.

The Phoenix Lights Abduction Incident: On March 13, 1997 (Age 29)

I just finished cooking dinner at 6:45 pm, when suddenly my two children, age 6 and age 8 come running into the house yelling "Mommy, mommy there are no more stars in the sky!!" Come look outside!

I'm outside and discovers that the stars are completely gone, I cannot make of what I'm seeing but it appears that the entire sky is covered with Perfectly aligned Rods, Nuts, Squares Bolts connect to one each other. As though being under the bottom of a well- made a car that covered the entire sky. The color of this thing is Black Dull color. That is just above the Tree Tops of my Apartment. If I threw a ball up in the air as far as I could the Ball would hit it easily. That's how close this thing was. I still didn't understand what I was looking at. I couldn't figure out So, I said to my children I was going to get to the corner to see how far this thing goes. So, I immediately run down to the corner and stop short thinking "wait a minute what the hell is this thing?" When suddenly I hear a calm voice say "Oh, go on. it's just us. "It's No Big Deal, go on and see how far this thing goes" Normally I would've said "What's no Big Deal? And Who's speaking"

And what am I looking at? But I didn't say any of that, I didn't even question what I heard. So, I run to the busy corner street. Before I get to the corner of Seventh Avenue and Roma (In between Camelback Mountain Rd and Indian School Rd) there's an alleyway connect to a nearby Texaco Gas Station with customers not noticing what's above their heads. Normally I would've gone right over there to get their attention to look up so they can tell me what I'm looking at because I didn't have a clue. I then noticed everything on the busy corner street is kind of going in slow motion. But I hear the normal sounds of cars going by, generators and such. I look down 7th Avenue to see how far this thing goes. It reaches all the way to the next city! I yell it out to my children "Wow, this thing reaches all the way towards Camelback mountain Wooow!

I then noticed my children were acting strange, normally they'd be standing right next to me asking me all kinds of questions. To the point, I'd have to tell them to be quiet and let me think. And, yet they were standing all the way at the front yard, walking towards the front door, no longer interested. Child 1 said: "Well I'm going in the house" while Child 2 follows right behind her. Shocked by their behavior I suddenly realize that this thing I'm looking at is a gigantic Mothership!! At that moment I knew somehow, I was taken by them before throughout my childhood. So, I'm Standing underneath this thing on the corner feeling alone and exposed. I said, "Oh Shit they Got Me" I decided not to look up at this Silent Massive Aircraft. Because at this point, I only want them to believe that I'm Dumb, Blind, and Useless and that I don't know anything. I don't want whoever is watching me know, that I know, what it is. I no longer can hear anything, no cars, no generator, no noise of "Anything at all" I then pretend I never saw anything and attempts to run towards my apartment. When suddenly everything around me turns into darkness. I cannot see my hand in front of me, I'm trying to feel for something in front of me when suddenly I completely black out.

This is very similar to what was above my apartment. Except there were no lights at all. Thousands of witnesses including a State Senator saw this ship that they claim had lights. The incident is shown on YouTube called "The Phoenix Lights".

After the incidence, I couldn't remember what had happened or how I got back into my apartment. In fact, not even the children could remember what happened during or after that entire incident until 13 years later!

And the way that I remembered was when I suddenly became almost obsessed with learning about Aliens and UFO'S in 2009. I suddenly started buying anything related to the subject. And the more I learned the more Knowledge thirsty I became. I never thought about UFO'S or Aliens before. Not even after my sister UFO Abduction during camp happened in the '70s. And in 2010, I stumbled across a YouTube news fed called "The Phoenix Lights" and that's when suddenly everything came flooding back into, I mind as if it happened yesterday! Holy Cow!

I immediately called my children and asked if they remembered and they too were Shocked and said "Oh my God yes! I remember mom, why didn't we talk about it when it happened??!" I asked them "what happened? And they both said, "Mom you came into the house late around 10:00 or 11:00 pm or later. Then you started to shut the windows and the blinds and told us not to go to the windows". But I don't remember doing that. And now that I asked them recently about what happened. On 2/2017 Child 1 cannot remember anything relating to that incident at all. Child 2 claims she remembers the incident. (Telling what happened in August 2018) Child 2 states that she was playing in the living room and suddenly heard someone in her head telling her happy to go outside and see that there are no more Stars in the Sky. As if it was an exciting event that was happening outside. Which promoted both Child 1 and Child 2 to go outside, as if Child 1 heard it too. They then returned to me with their sudden discovery that led to my abduction.

Since then I've been having reoccurring thoughts relating to the March 13 incidence. Which promote me to get some answers, mainly to see if anyone else was abducted beside me. I contacted MUFON a well- known UFO-Alien research department. I wrote a detailed description of all the Alien-UFO encounters that happened to me. MUFON Director immediately contacted me asking me pacifically about "The Phoenix Lights" they asked if I could go under hypnosis to retrieve the information. I informed them that I could not go under hypnosis and the reason for contacting MUFON was to see if anybody else was abducted and if so? What happened? And who were the people that were abducted? MUFON Director said he will check to see if anybody else was abducted. He found that no one else was taken but me. And express their concerns relating to me going on under. I still refuse to go under hypnosis. And till this day I occasionally receive emails from MUFON asking me to meet up with a well-known California Hypnotherapist named "Mrs. Smith."

I would like to know what happened, without me having someone else doing Hypnosis on me. So, I decided to learn how to do my own Hypnotherapy through deep meditation. And what I found is "Truly Extraordinary!

Triangle UFO Incident: April 2004 (Age 36)

I just moved into my apartment in Agoura Hills California. As I was standing on the balcony at night, I saw a Black Triangle UFO silently fly over my Apartment very close to the apartment. After I saw it, I can't remember anything after that. I don't think I even mentioned it the children at all.

UFO or Sun Incident: November 2007 (Age 39)

I was living in Los Angeles California, around 5:00 pm. I went out on my balcony and I saw what looked like the Sun right directly in front view and extremely Huge. But it wasn't the sun because I could look directly at it without squinting at all. And the real Sun was over to the far right. So, I called my kids to look at it. I noticed there were no cars and no people walking around outside at all. When my kids came to see what it was? After that, I can't remember anything else. And when I asked my children till this day 2/2017, they said they don't remember that incident at all.

August 2008 Dream Incident: (Age 40)

I had a dream, now my dreams are always shown as the **"Opposite"** of what is happening in real life. So, I dreamt that I'm standing up looking at this huge Sun that was directly in front of me. And there was a tall beautiful white man with blond hair and deep blue eyes. He was standing in front of the Sun as if he was part of the Sun. And I said, oh please tell me you're not a god or Jesus, because you're supposed to a Black person, how come your not Black? And he said, "I am the Arch Angel" [It was a name I can't remember like Arch Angel Uriel or Raphael.] But he kept repeating it to the point I said okay. (I got the impression that this Arch Angel is just a "Worker") And then he said, "I'm going to implant something inside you now" And he shot this bow and arrow into my navel. The arrow was a bright golden color. And when it went through my stomach, I felt no pain. Then darkness came upon me and within the darkness I heard voices say, "She can do anything, there's nothing she can't do, her powers are unlimited" While I heard this, I started floating from my bed up to the ceiling and through the roof flying happily into the nighttime sky and then I woke up.

Now let's intercepted this dream of what really happens. Instead of me standing up, I was laying down on a table or hospital bed looking at a medical light. While an Alien inserts a probe instrument into my Naval and took something out. Instead of me floating and flying in the nighttime sky, I was being brought back down through the ceiling onto my bed. Instead of having unlimited powers. Currently, on this planet, I have no powers.

Upper & Lower Back Incident: April 2011 (Age 43)

I Just moved to Hesperia California with my two children age 11 and age 8. We were getting ready for bed. {And no one else lived with us} Anyway we just moved into this house and we did not have any beds, so we slept on the floor with our comforters. I slept with my back towards the wall. And my children were sleeping directly in front of me and, we were laying down talking until we fell asleep. I then began to dream. And in my Dream, I dreamt that I woke up in the same position as to where we fell asleep but instead, we were sleeping inside of a Sun Porch. Like Back Patio Sun Porch. But we were in the Wilderness forestry area and I said "wow wake up guys we made it we're finally in the Forest! I was very happy because I am a Nature Freak!

As the kids were looking around, I noticed a Huge Floating Colorful Butterfly above the trees coming down very slowly through the trees. Then it turned into a Silver Metallic Butterfly that came closer to the point that I said" Oh it is coming down; oh, it's coming for me?? and now it's got me" and then everything went Black". When it went black in my dream? I then woke up in real life to someone shaking me as if someone was working on my Upper and Lower Back Spine. I heard drills, and Tool sounds. I felt and heard the movement of about 3 people or more working on me and, I was moving according to their pushes, pokes, and prods. While laying on my side in the same position as before.

I'm fully awake at this point so I turned to see who is tugging and pulling onto my Spine? And right when I did that a hand that I couldn't see kept his or her hand on my upper back shoulder and shoved me as to say "No"! don't look at us and be still" So I said "What? What are you doing? {Meanwhile, my children are still sleeping in the same position as before.} And then for some odd reason I said, "Well I'll just go back to sleep then" And everything went Black. When I woke up? I saw that my children were still sleeping and then a strong voice in my ear said, "Your Charkas are now in order, they are Rotating properly, Spinning accordingly in order now". Repeating it to the point where I said, "Okay Great, I got it, Thanks" And then the voice slowly faded until I could no longer hear it anymore.

Vanishing Birds or Cloaked Ship Incident: Fourth of July 2014 (Age 46)

Child 3 (age 14) and I went outside to see the fireworks. We then both looked to the right and saw 5 birds flying from a distance coming towards above our direction. I then said "well that's odd, what kind of Birds would fly at night? At that point, the birds were directly above us and then they all Vanished right before our eyes as if they were never there. Child 3 still remembers that incident today.

Child 2 and Child 3 Alien Encounters/Abductions

Child 2, from age 8 to about 13 have often told me that sometimes she finds herself having to play with other Children in this room were someone she cannot see watches over her. As she is assigned to play with an assortment of glowing floating or flying balls, shapes and sizes of colorful toys. Then she is placed inside this egg-shaped craft that she said is her "Personal world" inside this thing she is protected and very comfortable, she can go anywhere and do anything. She was there to learn how to fly and maneuver this egg-shaped Craft thing.

Child 3, newborn, March 10, 1999. I was just released from the hospital from giving Birth to my child 3, I was in my Apartment in Phoenix Az. I was sitting up in the bed holding her when two men walked in the room. One was taller than the other one and both were transparent looking. You could see right through them. They walked around to the front of the Bed and looked at her for a while. I then uncovered her blankets so they can get a better look at her arms, legs, face, etc. Once they saw that she was fine? They disappeared. I had no fear and didn't' think anything about it.

Child 3, Year 2010 age 11. We were living in Los Angeles and we both heard what sounded like a short drill, like a tool drill or landing gears on the roof of our Apartment around 8:00 pm. After we heard it, I went to bed for some odd reason and She went up to her room. Later that night around 2:00 in the morning I went upstairs to see about her, and she was standing in front of her bedroom window and told me that the Moon was very Orange and it moved from one direction to another back and forth. She then said that she comes from "The Brother Twin Planet" I said "What is that? And she said, "Its two planets located behind this Orange Moon" and that she uses to occupy or live there. I said "Who told you that? And she said, "The people that picked me up just now". I said do they always pick you up. And she said, "I can't remember but they will come again this week". And they did come later that week. Because She found herself on the other side of the bed on the floor with her stuffed animals neatly in a row as if someone placed them there on purpose. I do not know how she ended up that way when she's always tucked with the covers sealed underneath the mattress.

This Book is Dedicated to my #1 Wonderful Lovely Family;
Katherine Baby ISIS England, Cinamon Sweet, Starr Lee, Cuba Mane,
Dwight- You already know, "Stale and Sorry Ass Hell"

Conclusion

I hope you all enjoyed reading this book and as Always, the Promise Land is never too far from where you are. You just have to "Know" that it Exist.

Sincerely Yours Truly,
Katherine Irvin

www.ingramcontent.com/pod-product-compliance
Lightning Source LLC
Chambersburg PA
CBHW030742180526

45163CB00003B/896